SCIENTIFIC
AMERICAN™

CUTTING-EDGE SCIENCE™

21st-Century
Robotics

ROSEN
PUBLISHING®

New York

Published in 2007 by The Rosen Publishing Group, Inc.
29 East 21st Street, New York, NY 10010

The articles in this book first appeared in the pages of *Scientific American*,
as follows: "A New Race of Robots" by W. Wayt Gibbs, March 2004;
"The Spirit of Exploration" by George Musser, March 2004; "Controlling
Robots with the Mind" by Miguel A. L. Nicolelis and John K. Chapin,
October 2002; "An Army of Small Robots" by Robert Grabowski, Luis
E. Navarro-Serment, and Pradeep K. Khosla, November 2003; "Plug-and-
Play Robots" by W. Wayt Gibbs, April 2004; "Robots That Suck" by
George Musser, February 2003; "Long-Distance Robots" by Mark Alpert,
December 2001; "Kibbles and Bytes" by Mark Alpert, June 2001.

First Edition

Library of Congress Cataloging-in-Publication Data

21st-century robotics.—1st ed.
    p. cm.—(Scientific American cutting-edge science)
Includes index.
ISBN-13: 978-1-4042-0985-5
ISBN-10: 1-4042-0985-9 (library binding)
1. Robotics—Popular works. I. Scientific American. II. Title: Twentyfirst
century robotics.
TJ211.15.A14 2006
629.8'92—dc22

                                                          2006024275

Manufactured in the United States of America

On the cover: An up-close illustration of a millibot, or miniature robot,
which is no bigger than a Matchbox car.

Illustration credits: Cover, pp. 38, 39, 46, 62–64 © Bryan Christie Design;
p. 6 © W. Wayt Gibbs; p. 8 © Lucy Reading/Sources: MDEP, BLM, SRA/
DARPA; pp. 20, 21, 22 © Bryan Christie Design/Source: The Red Team;
pp. 28–29 © Alfred T. Kamajian/Source: NASA/JPL/Cornell University.

Contents

"A New Race of
I. Robots"

by W. Wayt Gibbs

Around the U.S., engineers are finishing one-year crash projects to create robots able to dash 200 miles through the Mojave Desert in a day, unaided by humans. Scientific American tailed the odds-on favorite team for 10 months and found that major innovations in robotics are not enough to win such a contest. Obsession is also required

PITTSBURGH, DECEMBER 10, 2003: A cold rain blows sideways through the night into the face of Chris Urmson as he frets over Sandstorm, the robotic vehicle idling next to him on an overgrown lot between two empty steel mills. Urmson checks a tarp protecting the metal cage full of computers and custom electronics that serves as the sensate head of the chimeric robot, which has the body of an old Marine Corps Humvee. His ungloved hands shivering and his body aching from three sleep-deprived days and nights of work in the field, Urmson stares glumly at the machine and weighs his options. None of them are good.

He and his teammates had vowed months ago that by midnight tonight Sandstorm would complete a 150-mile journey on its own. It seemed a reasonable goal at the time: after all, 150 miles on relatively smooth, level ground would be but a baby step toward the 200-mile, high-speed desert crossing that the robot must be ready for on March 13, 2004, if it is to win the U.S. Department of Defense's Grand Challenge race, as well as the $1-million prize and the prestige that accompanies an extraordinary leap in mobile robotics.

But after 20 hours of nonstop debugging, Sandstorm's navigational system is still failing in mystifying ways. Two days ago the machine was driving itself for miles at a time. Last night it crashed through a fence, and today it halts after just a few laps around the test path. The dozen or so team members here are wet, cold and frazzled, hunched over laptops in a makeshift lean-to or hunkered down in a van. The 28-year-old Urmson has hardly seen his wife and two-month-old baby for weeks. Continuing under these wretched conditions seems pointless.

On the other hand, an hour ago he and the rest of the group huddled around William "Red" Whittaker, the leader of the Red Team—and Urmson's Ph.D. adviser at Carnegie Mellon University (CMU)—and acceded to his decision that they would continue fixing and testing through the night and into the day and through the night again, if need be, until Sandstorm completed the 150-mile traverse they had promised. For the umpteenth time, Red repeated the team's motto: "We say what we'll do, and we do what we say." Their reputations, their morale—and for the students, their final-exam grades—are on the line.

But at the moment, Whittaker is not around, so Urmson, as the team's technical director, is in charge. He looks at the rivulets streaming over the tarp, considers

JANUARY 20: Sandstorm grows faster, smarter and more robust almost every day. Yet Whittaker still gives it only 40 percent odds of finishing the race.

The Competitors

MORE THAN 100 TEAMS registered for the Grand Challenge; 86 sent technical applications to DARPA, which approved 45. DARPA officials later culled the field to 25 vehicles, which fall into roughly four categories. No more than 20 will be allowed to race.

Modified All-Terrain Vehicles

Pros: Inexpensive; off-road suspensions are standard; can stop, turn and accelerate quickly; small size provides a margin of error on narrow trails.
Cons: Sensors are low and thus limited in their range of view; high risk of critical damage in a collision; very limited ability to generate electrical power; small fuel tanks; overturn easily.
Teams: ENSCO, Phantasm, Virginia Tech

Modified Sport-Utility Vehicles

Pros: Easily acquired; good ground clearance; large enclosed interior for electronics; powerful engines; high mounting points for sensors.
Cons: Expensive; high rollover risk; complex electrical system; suspension is designed for paved roads rather than trails.

Teams: Arctic Tortoise, Axion Racing, Caltech, Digital Auto Drive, Insight Racing, Navigators, Overbot, Palos Verdes Road Warriors

Dune Buggies
Pros: Very low center of gravity prevents overturning; frame and suspension are customized for desert racing; lightweight, agile and fast.
Cons: Sensors are low and vulnerable to collisions and dust; small wheels; low mass and electrical budgets limit onboard computing.
Teams: AI Motorvator, CyberRider, LoGHIQ, Sciautonics (which is fielding two robots)

Modified Military Vehicles
Pros: Very high ground clearance, stability and crash tolerance; powerful engines and large chassis can easily carry a large payload of electronics and computers; high vantage point for sensors.
Cons: Expensive and hard to obtain; parts are difficult to find; stiff suspension creates problems for sensors; wide turning radius; relatively slow acceleration and braking.
Teams: The Red Team, Terramax

how many weeks of work could be undone by one leak shorting the circuits inside, and aborts the test, sending everyone home to their beds.

The next day brings hell to pay. Like an angry coach at halftime, Whittaker castigates the team for giving up and for missing other self-imposed goals. "A great deal of what we agreed to do got lost as the team focused monotonically on the 150-mile objective," he rebukes. "The vehicle body didn't get painted; the Web site didn't get updated; the sensor electronics weren't completed. And do we win the race if we don't have better shock isolation than we have now?" Heads shake. "No, we'll lose the race. Is the condition of this shop consistent with who we are?" he asks, waving at

The Grand Challenge Race

DARPA ANNOUNCED in February 2003 that it was organizing a desert race for self-navigating robotic vehicles to be held on March 13, 2004. The race was named the Grand Challenge because its requirements—cross 200 miles of unfamiliar, rough terrain in 10 hours or less, without any human assistance—fell well beyond the capabilities of any robot yet designed.

THE PRIZE: $1 million to the team whose vehicle completes the course in the shortest time less than 10 hours.

THE RULES: The robotic racers must be fully autonomous; during the race they cannot receive signals of any kind (except a stop command) from humans. The vehicles must stay on the ground and within the boundaries of the course. No robot may intentionally interfere with another. The race will begin with a staggered start; a qualifying event will determine who goes first. If no vehicle wins in 2004, the race will be repeated each year until there is a winner or the funding runs out (after 2007).

THE COURSE: Two hours before the race begins, DARPA officials will give each team a CD-ROM containing a series of GPS coordinates, called waypoints, spaced 150 to 1,000 feet apart. The width of the route between waypoints will also vary: in some sections of the course, racers will have to remain within a 10-foot-wide corridor, whereas in other sections they will be able to roam more freely. Depending on how officials mix and match from various potential routes through the Mojave Desert (map), the course may be as short as 150 miles or as long as 210 miles.

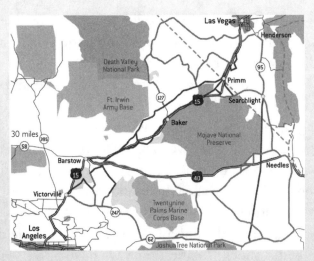

RACE OFFICIALS have warned participants to expect sandy trails, narrow underpasses, power line towers and hairpin turns. The Red Team is creating a test course in Pittsburgh that includes all of these hazards.

the tools and parts scattered over every flat surface. Eyes avert. He clenches his jaw.

"Yesterday we lost that sense deep inside of what we're all about," Whittaker continues. "What we have just been through was a dress rehearsal of race day. This is exactly what the 13th of March will be like. We're in basic training; this is all about cranking it up a notch. Come March, *we* will be the machine, an impeccable machine."

Whittaker concludes his pep talk and asks for a show of hands of all those willing to devote every minute of the next four days to another grueling attempt to complete a 15-hour, 150-mile autonomous traverse. Fourteen hands shoot up. Sometime between the first team meeting eight months ago and today, each person in the room had passed his own point of no return.

A Grand Challenge Indeed

APRIL 30, 2003: In a conference room at CMU's Robotics Institute, a tall man rises to his feet. He wears the blue blazer and tan chinos of an academic but has the bravado of a heavyweight who used to box for the marines. "Welcome to the first meeting of the Red Team," he booms. "I'm Red Whittaker, director of the Fields Robotics Center, and I am committed to leading this team to victory in Las Vegas next year."

Whittaker attended the conference last February at which officials from the Defense Advanced Research Projects Agency (DARPA) announced their first-ever prize contest, a robot race from Barstow, Calif., to Las Vegas [*see box on page 8*]. DARPA set up the competition to spur progress toward a vehicle that could enter a battlefield with minimal human supervision. "It could be delivering supplies or taking out wounded. It could also be a tank," says Anthony J. Tether, the agency's director.

A different vision moved Whittaker to be among the first of more than 100 teams that would sign up to enter the race. To him, the principal attractions are the public attention it will bring to robotics and the difficulty of the task, which he often compares to Lindbergh's first transatlantic flight. "The race defies prevailing technology, and many hold that the challenge prize is unwinnable in our time," he wrote in an e-mail on March 13 to potential volunteers and sponsors.

Building an autonomous robot would not be the hard part. With colleagues at the Robotics Institute, Whittaker has created self-driving vehicles that haul boulders, harvest crops, map underground mines, and hunt for meteorites in Antarctica. What makes the Grand Challenge aptly named is its speed—the speed at which the robot must move over rough, unfamiliar terrain and the haste with which it must be built.

"In order to win, Sandstorm will have to average better than 10 meters per second [22 miles per hour]," CMU engineer Scott Thayer points out. That is roughly 10 times the speed of the prototype robots that DARPA has acquired through a four-year, $22-million program to develop unmanned ground vehicles.

"Just getting it to move that fast will be a profoundly challenging problem," Thayer says. "Maintaining those speeds safely for almost 10 hours straight is just mind-boggling." He ventures that "it will take a fundamental innovation to win. And the professional roboticists like me may be the last to come up with a breakthrough like that. After doing this for decades, we tend to think more incrementally. So who knows—one person with a dune buggy may win it."

Blueprint for the Red Team

JUNE 24: "The last time we met, we considered a tricycle with giant wheels seven feet in diameter," Whittaker reports at the team's third meeting. "We also looked at a four-wheel-drive, four-wheel-steered vehicle with a chassis that can change shape. We gave these hard technical looks, but each is too bold a technical step for a yearlong program."

Three months into that year, the team has not yet decided whether to base its robot on a tortoise, such as a military Humvee, or on a hare, such as a professional pickup truck or a low-slung Chenowth combat buggy. Whittaker presents a mathematical analysis of how each vehicle would perform on a course composed mainly of dirt roads and rough trails. "A tough consistent vehicle could go 250 miles in 9.3 hours; a sprinter would take 10.6 hours," he concludes. The choice seems clear, yet it will be September before they will raise the door on the Planetary Robotics Building, where the team has set up shop, and push in a 1986 Hummer M998.

But the group—which now numbers more than 50, thanks to the dozens of CMU graduate and undergraduate students working on the project for credit—has prepared a 58-page technical paper describing how Sandstorm will track its position, plan its route, and detect and avoid hazards in its way. Alex Gutierrez, one of the graduate students at the core of the team, hands out copies to executives from SAIC, Boeing, Caterpillar, Seagate and other corporate partners as they enter the room.

"First we will work for eight months to create the best possible maps of the course terrain," Whittaker explains. "When DARPA hands out the race route, two hours before the race starts, we will use those maps to calculate the optimal route and do a simulated flight though it." The resulting list of thousands of GPS coordinates will be copied to computers on the robot, giving it "little seeds of corn to aim for every meter or so," Whittaker says. "Sandstorm will just go along like Pac-Man, gobbling up these little virtual dots."

The budget now sums to an astonishing bottom line: $3,539,491. Nearly $2.5 million of that is for personnel expenses that will probably never get paid. The $725,000 for the vehicle itself is not optional, however, and so far only Caterpillar and a local foundation have written checks. But many others are donating valuable equipment and expertise.

Applanix, for example, delivered a $60,000 position-tracking system that not only will allow Sandstorm to know where it is as it bounces along the desert but also will help it to solve one of the toughest problems in mobile robotics: watching where it is going with a steady gaze. "It will know what the world outside looks like through lasers, what it looks like in radar, and what it looks like through a stereo, or two-eyed, camera—provided by our good friends at SAIC," Whittaker declares. Each of these sensors will be mounted on motorized platforms connected to the Applanix system in a tight feedback loop. These gimbals, as engineers call them, will compensate for the motion of the vehicle much like the neck and eye muscles of a human driver.

Many of the competing teams have similar plans. One composed of undergraduates at the California Institute of Technology is forgoing radar and relying heavily on four video cameras mounted to the front of their modified Chevrolet Tahoe. The Red Team's Navtech radar is worth its $47,000 price because "it works through dust, which can blind the other sensors," Whittaker says. For that very reason, Ohio State University's Team Terramax is mounting two radars—plus six cameras and four laser scanners—on the robot it is building from a huge six-wheeled Oshkosh truck.

More sensors are not necessarily better. Each one streams data like a fire hose; too many can choke a robot's computers. As the vehicle jolts and shakes, overlapping scans may confuse more than they inform.

And merging sensor data of different types is notoriously tricky. Laser scanners produce "point clouds," radars emit rectangular blips, a stereo camera generates a so-called disparity map. "If you aren't careful," says Jay Gowdy, a CMU scientist on the Red Team, "you can end up combining the weaknesses of each sensor instead of combining their strengths."

Reality Checks In

NOVEMBER 6: Whittaker, Urmson and Philip Koon, one of two engineers that Boeing Phantom Works has embedded with the team, sit down for the weekly teleconference with the team's partners. "We were maybe 50–50 on our goals this week—this is the first time we have really missed the mark," Whittaker announces. The radar was hung up in customs en route from the U.K. After more than 100 hours of work, the mapping group has completed less than 4 percent of the area they aim to cover. And money is getting tight. "At the moment, we're short about $950,000 and burning through eight grand a day," Whittaker reports. He hopes to sell advertising space on the robot's hood and fin for half a million dollars but has found no buyers.

Two weeks later the team meets to confront other problems. A superprecise optical odometer built to slide on the robot's axle does not fit together properly. "And this is troubling," Whittaker says as he points to a large spike on a graph of how the computer cage— they call it the E-box—bounced around as the vehicle ran over a railroad tie at five miles an hour. "That reads seven *g*'s, which is very bad," he continues. Hard disks will crash and chips may pop from their sockets unless the E-box is isolated from all shocks greater than about three *g*'s. They must figure out a better way to suspend the E-box within the chassis.

"Engineering is always a series of failures to get to success," points out Bryon Smith, one of the few seasoned roboticists on the team. "It takes iteration after iteration to get it right." But iterations take time. The 100 days that Whittaker scheduled for development are almost up, and the team has yet to install and wire all the onboard computers, construct the gimbals, finish the software or mount the sensors.

"This vehicle hasn't rolled so much as a foot under its own control," Whittaker says. "You have promised to get 150 miles on that beast in two weeks. Just so we're clear on the ambition here: DARPA's Spinner vehicle program, based right here at CMU, has a team of pros and a budget of $5 million and is now in its second year. So far the furthest it has driven is 15 miles. Okay, anyone who thinks it is not appropriate for us to go for 150 miles by December 10, raise your hand." No one does. "There it is," he smiles. "We're now heading into that violent and wretched time of birthing this machine and launching it on its maiden voyage."

DECEMBER 1: "There were a bunch of us here all day on Thanksgiving and through the weekend—me, Alex, Philip, Yu [Kato] and several others. But it was worth it," Urmson says. So ends any semblance of normal life as these young engineers are drawn into their leader's constructive obsession. "Around 3 or 4 A.M. Sunday morning, as all the pieces started coming together and getting connected, it felt damn good," Whittaker adds, casting critical looks at those who spent the holiday with their families.

The robot now has several of its sensory organs attached and a rudimentary nervous system working. Smith and Kato have assembled the three-axis gimbal that will aim and steady the stereo camera and long-range laser only to discover "very strange behavior with the fiber-optic gyroscopes" that measure the device's motion, Smith reports. Whittaker listens intently to the details. "The gimbal is an essential device to win the race," he reminds the team. "Its main purpose is to suppress jitter. Right now when we turn it on, it induces jitter." For the next week, Kato will hardly leave the shop as he valiantly attempts to correct through software a fundamental flaw in the gyroscope hardware.

At 7:51 the next evening, after handling well in a piloted test run, Sandstorm is allowed to take its own wheel. It is driving blind, simply following a recorded list of GPS waypoints that trace an oval loop. The computer is doing the steering, but Urmson is on board as a "human kill switch," to hit the emergency stop button if something goes wrong. Four miles and half an hour later programmer Kevin Peterson clicks a button on his laptop, a command travels wirelessly to the robot, and Sandstorm brakes to a halt. "Very well done," Whittaker congratulates, and sends the vehicle back to the shop for another night of modifications.

"From now on we need everybody here 24 hours so that as soon as the vehicle returns from the field, people jump on it and start working," Whittaker says in the morning. "It is exciting to see a robot first spring into action. But the point is to make this kind of driving boring. A 150-mile traverse in the next five days, while taking sensor data: that's the final exam, and it's pass/fail."

DECEMBER 8: The Red Team has set up camp by the empty blast furnaces to watch the robot make its 15-hour nonstop, unguided journey. They record a figure-eight test path, but the machine gets confused at the crossing point; sometimes it goes left and sometimes right. So they go back to the oval loop.

But before the test can begin, a short circuit sends current surging through a wireless "E-stop" receiver that DARPA has provided so that race officials can disable any robot that goes berserk. With that receiver fried, the team has no fail-safe way to force Sandstorm to stop—only a piece of software. Peterson and Martin Stolle, two of the team's software gurus, urge Whittaker not to rely on the software.

Urmson arrives with a servomotor borrowed from a radio-controlled airplane and proceeds to jury-rig a wireless kill switch. But that transmitter also shorts out. "So now we have just Martin's software stop," Whittaker sighs. "Martin, how many hours do you have on your controller?" he asks.

"We've tested it for about half an hour," Martin replies. Moreover, he warns, if the onboard computer fails, "we will lose all control, and the vehicle will just plow ahead until it hits an obstacle larger than a Humvee."

Urmson huddles the team together. "We can go ahead, but we all need to understand and agree that—"

"Everyone understands it, and I'm accountable," Red interrupts. "It's not a question of pros or cons; we're going to do it." The sun has set, and the slush on the track is refreezing. Whittaker insists that two team members stay in the open to keep watch as the robot drives 792 laps around its short test loop.

With a puff of gray smoke, Sandstorm zooms forward. As it rounds the first two turns and enters a straightaway, sparks appear in the undercarriage. It skids to a stop on command, and team members sprint out with a fire extinguisher. The cause is innocuous: someone had forgotten to refill a gas cylinder that keeps the parking brake released, so it was driving with its brake on. They push the vehicle back onto the course, only to find that the batteries have failed.

And so it went for the next several days, with one thing after another going wrong. While Smith and Kato managed to conquer the bugs in the gimbal and get one of its three arms working for 15 hours, gremlins bedeviled the rest of the Red Team, sending Sandstorm careening into, and later through, a chain-link fence. In the wee hours of December 13, the robot was just clearing 119 miles when it headed for the hills and had to be stopped. They persisted for two more days, through a snowstorm and bitter cold, persisted and failed.

Sprinting to the Starting Line

DECEMBER 21: "We didn't do the 150," Whittaker acknowledges, as the diehards meet to take stock. "But it was a hell of a four days. It was our battle cry, and it was magnificent."

On Christmas Eve a new shock isolation design for the E-box is tested. It works, as do all three arms on the gimbal. Christmas Day brings—what else?—test, fail, rework, repeat.

Within two weeks, as industry partners fly in for the last full team meeting on January 6, the robot is ready for its public unveiling before politicians and television cameras. Behind closed doors, Whittaker acknowledges that "in the last six months we've fallen behind a month. Following GPS waypoints, the vehicle is now rock-solid, to the point where you can turn your back on it." Sandstorm has graduated from a paved lot to an open field, where it now safely drives by itself at more than 30 miles an hour.

But although the machine can see the world, it cannot yet reason enough to avoid obstacles. Even with 10 of the most powerful processors that Intel makes installed in Sandstorm, the computers formulate their plans about a third too slowly.

How Sandstorm Works

JUST BEFORE THE RACE BEGINS, the Red Team will calculate the best route and send a detailed itinerary (in the form of geographic coordinates for every meter of the course) to the Sandstorm robot. The vehicle will try to follow this virtual trail of breadcrumbs from the starting line to the finish as closely as it can, while detecting and avoiding any unexpected obstacles, such as a disabled racer in the road ahead. To succeed, the robot must solve four challenging problems.

I. TRACKING ITS POSITION

An Applanix navigation computer contains two GPS receivers, three fiber-optic gyroscopes, three silicon accelerometers and an ultraprecise odometer, which it uses to pin down the robot's position to within 50 centimeters and to measure its orientation in space to 0.4 degree. The system updates the robot's sense of where it is 200 times a second.

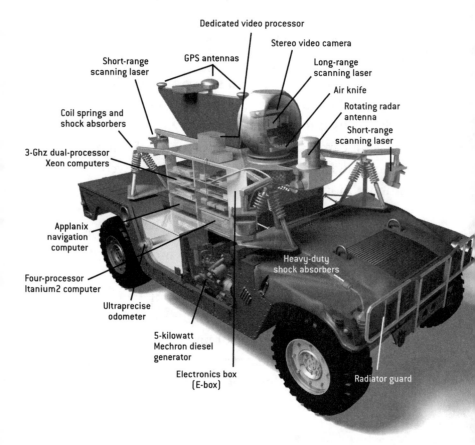

2. PERCEIVING AN OBSTACLE

Sandstorm uses four kinds of sensors to look for obstacles (*a*). A long-range laser traces the profile of the terrain 50 times a second. Successive profiles build up to form a 3-D model (*b*). Shorter-range lasers also cover all sides of the vehicle. A stereo camera sends video to a dedicated computer that estimates the slope and roughness of the ground. A rotating radar antenna will pick up obstructions (*c*) even when dust or glare blinds the other sensors.

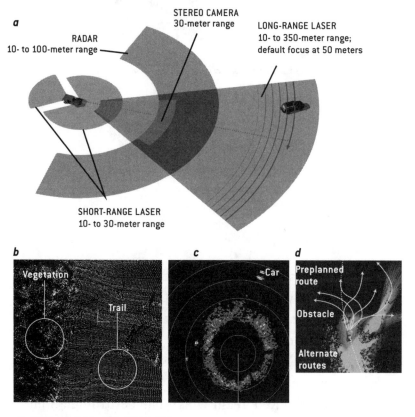

a

STEREO CAMERA
30-meter range

LONG-RANGE LASER
10- to 350-meter range;
default focus at 50 meters

RADAR
10- to 100-meter range

SHORT-RANGE LASER
10- to 30-meter range

b

Vegetation

Trail

c

Car

d

Preplanned route

Obstacle

Alternate routes

3. REVISING ITS ROUTE

Even the best maps are not up to the minute. So three onboard Xeon computers will use data from each sensor to update the "cost" assigned to each square meter in the area. A paved road carries a cost of zero; a cliff or competing racer warrants an infinite cost. Several times a second, a fourth Itanium2 computer checks whether the "breadcrumb trail" (*d*) passes through high-cost territory. If so, the planner program prices alternative routes and shifts the breadcrumbs to the shortest safe path.

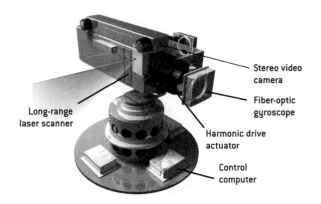

Stereo video camera

Fiber-optic gyroscope

Long-range laser scanner

Harmonic drive actuator

Control computer

4. ENDURING THE DUST AND BUMPS

Back roads through the Mojave are rough, so the team has equipped the Humvee with racing shocks and springs, a radiator guard and run-flat wheels. To protect the computers, the electronics box is suspended on tripods of spring-reinforced shock absorbers and strapped in place by superstrong bungee cords. A dozen "ruggedized" hard disks inside will operate in redundant pairs. As Sandstorm bounces over a washboard dirt road at 30 miles an hour, it must hold its forward sensors steady. Red Team engineers built a computer-controlled stabilizer, or gimbal (*above*), that both aims and steadies the camera and long-range laser. The gimbal uses three fiber-optic gyroscopes and three precise actuators to measure and compensate for the vehicle's pitch, roll and yaw. The radar is similarly bolted to a one-axis gimbal.

In February the robot and its creators will head to the desert. "We need to put 10,000 miles of testing on it," Whittaker says. "This fancy stuff could shake apart because it's all prototype. Just inside the E-box there are 5,000-odd components, a failure in any one of which could screw us up. Any team could beat us."

And if the Red Team wins? The best thing about building a new race of robots, Whittaker said one frigid night in December as we watched Sandstorm do its laps beneath a nearly perfect full moon, is not the act of creation. "What's most fun is exploring the space

of possibilities you have opened with your invention.
I'm thinking about proposing a mission to NASA to
launch a lunar rover that could circumnavigate the
pole of the moon, searching for ice." Other team
members have suggested building a robot to run the
Iditarod in Alaska or to serve as an ambulance in
Antarctica.

More likely, however, the $1-million prize will go
unclaimed this year and the contest will repeat in 2005.
"If no one wins this race and we recommit for next year,
who's in?" Whittaker asks at the end of the meeting.
Up go a roomful of hands.

More To Explore

The Red Team Web site: **redteamracing.org**
For links to other teams: **www.darpa.mil/grandchallenge/
    teams.htm**
For more information on the Grand Challenge race:
    www.darpa.mil/grandchallenge/

The Author

Senior writer *W. WAYT GIBBS* has been in Pittsburgh
covering the progress of the Red Team since March 2003.

"The Spirit of
2. Exploration"

by George Musser

NASA's rover fights the curse of the Angry Red Planet

At 8:15 P.M. Pacific time on January 3, the Spirit rover, tucked inside its protective capsule, separated from its interplanetary mother ship and prepared to enter the atmosphere of Mars. For weeks, mission engineers and scientists had been listing in grim detail everything that could go wrong. Explosive bolts might not blow on time; strong winds might slam the capsule against the ground; the lander might settle with its nose down, wedged helplessly between rocks; radio links might fail. As the final days ticked by, a dust storm on the planet erupted, reducing the density of the upper atmosphere. To compensate, controllers reprogrammed the parachute to deploy earlier. Eight hours before the capsule's entry, deputy mission manager Mark Adler said, "We're sending a complicated system into an unknown environment at very high speed. I feel calm. I feel ready. I can only conclude it's because I don't have a full grasp of the situation."

This candid doom-mongering was reassuring. If the team had said there was nothing to worry about, it would have been time to start worrying. Between 1960 and 2002 the U.S., Russia and Japan sent 33 missions to the Red Planet. Nine made it. By the standards of planetary exploration, the failure rate is not unusually high: of the first 33 missions to the moon, only 14 succeeded. But the blunders that damned the Mars Climate Orbiter in 1999—neglecting to convert imperial to metric units, then failing to diagnose the error when the spacecraft kept drifting off course—are hard to live down. And just a week before Spirit reached Mars, the British Beagle 2 lander bounded into the Martian atmosphere never to be heard from again.

Controllers at NASA's Jet Propulsion Laboratory (JPL) have a tradition of opening a bag of peanuts for good luck, and the moment had come to do so. At 8:29 P.M., Spirit started its meteoric descent. (To be precise, that is when the confirmation signal reached Earth. By then, Spirit had already landed on Mars; the only question was whether it had landed in one piece or in many.) Within two minutes, the lander had survived the peak atmospheric heating and maximum g-force. After another two minutes, it deployed its chute and emerged from its capsule. Two minutes later its cushion of air bags inflated and controllers announced, "We have signs of bouncing on the surface of Mars."

The control room became a blur of cheering and hugging. It didn't take long, though, for people to wonder whether they had cheered and hugged too soon. The radio signal had flatlined. Rob Manning, the leader of the group that devised the landing sequence, recalls: "The signal disappeared. That caused us some pause. I was trying to act calm. It was nerve-wracking." Up until then, he says, the entry had felt just like one of the team's many test runs. "It was only when the signal started going away that I said, 'Uh-oh, this is not a rehearsal.'"

Engineers had warned that Spirit might go silent for 10 minutes or so until it rolled to a stop. A tumbling lander does not make a good transmission platform. But the 10th minute came and went without contact, then the 11th and the 12th. People swiveled in their chairs, crossed their arms, chewed gum. A thin jittery line, representing radio static, ran across the bottom of controllers' computer screens. Manning says he was watching the bottom of his screen so intently that it took him a moment to notice when the line jumped to the top. At 8:52 P.M., or 2:51 P.M. local time at the landing site, Spirit proclaimed its safe arrival on the Red Planet.

Squyres's Odyssey

LIKE SAILORS ROUNDING Cape Horn, scientists and engineers willingly put themselves in the capricious hands of fate for a reason: to put life on our planet into context, either as a singular phenomenon or as an exemplar of a universal process. Steve Squyres, principal investigator of the rover's scientific instruments, has been trying to get to Mars for 17 years. The Cornell University professor has something of a wunderkind reputation. He did his Ph.D. from start to finish in three years and, during the 1980s, became an expert on half the solid bodies of the solar system, from the icy satellites of

Jupiter to the volcanic plains of Venus to the water-cut highlands of Mars. But he came to feel that his career was missing something.

"The real advances in our business come from people who build instruments and put them on spacecraft and send them to the planets," he says. "I worked on Voyager; I worked on Magellan. I didn't think of those missions, I didn't design those instruments, I didn't calibrate them. I just parachuted in at the end, scooped up some data and went off and wrote a bunch of papers. It was a very enjoyable, satisfying way to do a career, in a lot of respects, but I did feel that I was profiting by the efforts of others. For just once—and it is going to be just once; this is an experience neither to be missed nor repeated—for just once I wanted to do one where at the end I could say, You know, okay, that was something that I helped make happen."

In 1987 Squyres put together a team, built a camera and proposed it to NASA for what became the Mars Pathfinder mission. It had the wrong dimensions and was disqualified. He also joined one of the instrument teams for the Mars Observer spacecraft. Shortly after it lifted off in September 1992, its booster rocket fired to break out of Earth orbit, and the fragility of spaceflight intruded. The radio signal went dead. Sitting in the auditorium at launch control, Squyres put his head in his hands and said, "I think we may have lost it. I think we may have lost it." Forty minutes later the spacecraft reappeared. It vanished for good when it got to Mars the following year.

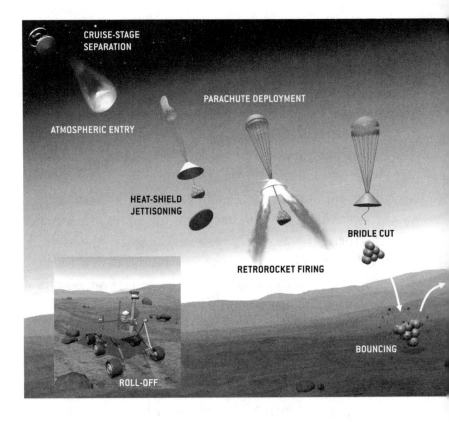

CRUISE-STAGE SEPARATION

ATMOSPHERIC ENTRY

PARACHUTE DEPLOYMENT

HEAT-SHIELD JETTISONING

RETROROCKET FIRING

BRIDLE CUT

BOUNCING

ROLL-OFF

In 1993 Squyres and his team proposed another instrument package and were again turned down. As they were developing yet another set of plans, for a full-blown mobile geology lab called Athena, news broke that a meteorite discovered in Antarctica might contain hints of past life on Mars. The hoopla reenergized Mars exploration. The Pathfinder mission in 1997 showed what a rover could do, and in November of that year NASA gave the go-ahead to Athena. Squyres found himself the leader of 170 scientists and 600 engineers.

LANDING SEQUENCE of the Spirit rover followed the pattern pioneered by Mars Pathfinder in 1997. Spirit entered the atmosphere at 5.4 kilometers a second. Drag on the heat shield reduced its speed to 430 meters a second, the parachute slowed it to 70 meters a second, and rockets brought it to rest seven meters above the ground. (The rockets did not bring it all the way down, because that would have required extremely precise distance measurements and finely tuned rocket control.) Protected by air bags, Spirit bounced 28 times and came to rest about 300 meters southeast of the point of first impact.

PETAL OPENING

ROVER PREPARATION

Two years later NASA lost the Mars Climate Orbiter and the Mars Polar Lander. Although Squyres's team was not directly involved, the fiascoes convulsed the entire Mars program. In response to an investigation panel, which put the blame largely on a caustic mix of underfunding and overconfidence, the agency increased the budget for the rovers; they eventually cost $820 million. Redesigned and refocused, Spirit and its twin, Opportunity, finally blasted off last summer. "To get through something like what we went through, you have to be optimistic by nature," Squyres says. "To be prepared for every eventuality, you also have to be pessimistic by nature."

Freeze-Dried Planet

AS THE TWO Mars Exploration Rovers (MERs) were coming together, Martian science went through an upheaval. The Mariner and Viking missions of the 1960s and 1970s revealed a cold, dry and lifeless world, but one etched with remnants of past vigor: delicate valley networks from the distant past and vast flood channels from the intermediate past. Researchers expected that when new space probes assayed the planet, they would find water-related minerals: carbonates, clays, salts.

Over the past six and a half years, the Mars Global Surveyor and Mars Odyssey orbiters—bearing duplicates of the instruments that the ill-fated Mars Observer carried—have looked for and detected essentially none of those minerals. They have found layers of olivine, a mineral that liquid water should have degraded. And yet the orbiters have also seen fresh gullies, old lake beds and shorelines, and an iron oxide mineral, gray hematite (as opposed to red hematite, otherwise known as rust), that typically forms in liquid water. The planet holds extensive reservoirs of ice and bears the marks of recent geologic and glacial activity. Scientists are more baffled than ever.

"There's a fairly raging debate about how the environment of early Mars differed from now," says Matt Golombek, the JPL planetary geologist who led the Pathfinder science team and is a member of the Mars Exploration Rover team. "MER is really the first attempt to go to the surface and try to verify what the environment was really like."

The notoriously risk-averse Viking planners sent their two landers to the most boring places on Mars. (To be fair, you'd probably do the same if you had a $3.5-billion, easily toppled spacecraft and knew almost nothing about the terrain.) Pathfinder, though bolder, was really just a test flight. Beyond a desire to study as many different rocks as possible, Golombek's team didn't much care where it went. Spirit and Opportunity are the first landers to visit places that scientists actively wanted to go.

From orbit, Spirit's new home, Gusev Crater, looks like a lake bed. It has fine layering, deltalike deposits and sinuous terracing, and it sits at the northern end of Ma'adim Vallis, one of the largest valleys on the planet. Opportunity has gone for the gray hematite, which is concentrated in Meridiani Planum. Phil Christensen, a planetary geologist at Arizona State University, recently studied the topography of the hematite outcrops and concluded that the mineral forms a thin, flat layer—as though Meridiani, like Gusev, was once a lake bed.

Only on the surface can these hypotheses be tested. For instance, because wind cannot transport sand grains larger than half a centimeter, the discovery of bigger grains would imply another agent of erosion, probably water. When hematite crystallizes in lake water (as opposed to, say, a hot spring), the chemical reaction often involves the mineral goethite, which spectrometers on the rovers can look for. Piece by piece, datum by datum, the rovers should help resolve how Mars can be both so Earth-like and so alien.

Mars under the Earthlings

ABOUT THREE HOURS after Spirit landed, at 11:30 P.M. Pacific time on January 3, the data started to pour in, relayed by the Odyssey orbiter. For observers used to earlier missions, when images slowly built up line by line like a curtain rising on another world, it was startling. The first pictures flashed up on the screen, and Gusev Crater leapt into the control room.

The main cameras sit on a mast 1.5 meters tall, so the view closely matches what you'd see if you stood on the planet. But it still takes some getting used to. Jim Bell, a Cornell scientist who has worked on the color panoramic camera, Pancam, since 1994, says: "One thing that I learned through all the testing we did is when you experience a place through the eyes of a rover, and then go yourself, it's pretty different. The sense of depth is very different, because you're looking at this flat projection of the world, and there's nothing in it for human reference. There's no trees, no fire hydrants—you're missing all the cues we have all around us that tell us how far away things are."

Even so, the first images have an eerily familiar quality, showing rocks, hollows, hills and mesas. "It's beautiful in the same way the desert is beautiful," aerospace engineer Julie Townsend says. "It's a beautiful vacantness, the beauty of an undisturbed landscape."

But space exploration is like plucking the petals of a daisy: it works, it works not, it works, it works not. You never know how it will end. Early morning Pacific time on January 21, controllers were preparing Spirit to analyze its first rock, named Adirondack. They instructed the rover to test part of the infrared spectrometer, and Spirit sent the robotic equivalent of "roger." But then it went silent. For two days, controllers tried nearly a dozen times to reach it. When they finally reestablished contact, the situation was serious. Though in no imminent danger, Spirit had rebooted itself more than 60 times trying to shake off a fault it could not diagnose. Pete Theisinger, the project manager, says, "The chances it will be perfect again are not good." But he adds, "The chances that it will not work at all are also low." And that, in the business of planetary science, is a victory.

The Author

GEORGE MUSSER, a staff writer, was a graduate student of Steve Squyres' in the early 1990s. For updates on the Spirit and Opportunity missions, see www.sciam.com

"Controlling Robots
3. with the Mind"

by Miguel A. L. Nicolelis and John K. Chapin

*People with nerve or limb injuries may one day be able
to command wheelchairs, prosthetics and even paralyzed
arms and legs by "thinking them through" the motions*

Belle, our tiny owl monkey, was seated in her
special chair inside a soundproof chamber at our Duke
University laboratory. Her right hand grasped a joystick
as she watched a horizontal series of lights on a display
panel. She knew that if a light suddenly shone and she
moved the joystick left or right to correspond to its
position, a dispenser would send a drop of fruit juice
into her mouth. She loved to play this game. And she
was good at it.

Belle wore a cap glued to her head. Under it were
four plastic connectors. The connectors fed arrays of
microwires—each wire finer than the finest sewing
thread—into different regions of Belle's motor cortex,
the brain tissue that plans movements and sends
instructions for enacting the plans to nerve cells in
the spinal cord. Each of the 100 microwires lay beside
a single motor neuron. When a neuron produced an
electrical discharge—an "action potential"—the
adjacent microwire would capture the current and
send it up through a small wiring bundle that ran
from Belle's cap to a box of electronics on a table
next to the booth. The box, in turn, was linked to

two computers, one next door and the other half a country away.

In a crowded room across the hall, members of our research team were getting anxious. After months of hard work, we were about to test the idea that we could reliably translate the raw electrical activity in a living being's brain—Belle's mere thoughts—into signals that could direct the actions of a robot. Unknown to Belle on this spring afternoon in 2000, we had assembled a multijointed robot arm in this room, away from her view, that she would control for the first time. As soon as Belle's brain sensed a lit spot on the panel, electronics in the box running two real-time mathematical models would rapidly analyze the tiny action potentials produced by her brain cells. Our lab computer would convert the electrical patterns into instructions that would direct the robot arm. Six hundred miles north, in Cambridge, Mass., a different computer would produce the same actions in another robot arm, built by Mandayam A. Srinivasan, head of the Laboratory for Human and Machine Haptics (the Touch Lab) at the Massachusetts Institute of Technology. At least, that was the plan.

If we had done everything correctly, the two robot arms would behave as Belle's arm did, at exactly the same time. We would have to translate her neuronal activity into robot commands in just 300 milliseconds— the natural delay between the time Belle's motor cortex planned how she should move her limb and the moment it sent the instructions to her muscles. If the brain of a living creature could accurately control two dissimilar robot arms—despite the signal noise and transmission delays inherent in our lab network and the error-prone Internet—perhaps it could someday control a mechanical device or actual limbs in ways that would be truly helpful to people.

Finally the moment came. We randomly switched on lights in front of Belle, and she immediately moved her joystick back and forth to correspond to them. Our robot arm moved similarly to Belle's real arm. So did Srinivasan's. Belle and the robots moved in synchrony, like dancers choreographed by the electrical impulses sparking in Belle's mind. Amid the loud celebration that erupted in Durham, N.C., and Cambridge, we could not help thinking that this was only the beginning of a promising journey.

In the two years since that day, our labs and several others have advanced neuroscience, computer science, microelectronics and robotics to create ways for rats, monkeys and eventually humans to control mechanical and electronic machines purely by "thinking through," or imagining, the motions. Our immediate goal is to help a person who has been paralyzed by a neurological disorder or spinal cord injury, but whose motor cortex is spared, to operate a wheelchair or a robotic limb. Someday the research could also help such a patient regain control over a natural arm or leg, with the aid of wireless communication between implants in the brain and the limb. And it could lead to devices that restore or augment other motor, sensory or cognitive functions.

The big question is, of course, whether we can make a practical, reliable system. Doctors have no means by which to repair spinal cord breaks or damaged brains. In the distant future, neuroscientists may be able to regenerate injured neurons or program stem cells (those capable of differentiating into various cell types) to take their place. But in the near future, brain-machine interfaces (BMIs), or neuroprostheses, are a more viable option for restoring motor function. Success this summer with macaque monkeys that completed different tasks than those we asked of Belle has gotten us even closer to this goal.

From Theory to Practice

RECENT ADVANCES in brain-machine interfaces are grounded in part on discoveries made about 20 years ago. In the early 1980s Apostolos P. Georgopoulos of Johns Hopkins University recorded the electrical activity of single motor-cortex neurons in macaque monkeys. He found that the nerve cells typically reacted most strongly when a monkey moved its arm in a certain direction. Yet when the arm moved at an angle away from a cell's preferred direction, the neuron's activity didn't cease; it diminished in proportion to the cosine of that angle. The finding showed that motor neurons were broadly tuned to a range of motion and that the brain most likely relied on the collective activity of dispersed populations of single neurons to generate a motor command.

Belle's 60-Mile Reach

On the day Belle first moved a multijointed robot arm with her thoughts, she wore a cap glued to her head. Beneath the cap, each of four plastic connectors fed an array of fine microwires into her cortex (a). As Belle saw lights shine suddenly and decided to move a joystick left or right to correspond to them, the microwires detected electrical signals produced by activated neurons in her cortex and relayed the signals to a "Harvey box" of electronics.

The box collected, filtered and amplified the signals and relayed them to a server computer in a room next door. The signals received by the box can be displayed as a raster plot (b);

Overview/ Brain Interfaces

- Rats and monkeys whose brains have been wired to a computer have successfully controlled levers and robot arms by imagining their own limb either pressing a bar or manipulating a joystick.
- These feats have been made possible by advances in microwires that can be implanted in the motor cortex and by the development of algorithms that translate the electrical activity of brain neurons into commands able to control mechanical devices.
- Human trials of sophisticated brain-machine interfaces are far off, but the technology could eventually help people who have lost an arm to control a robotic replacement with their mind or help patients with a spinal cord injury regain control of a paralyzed limb.

a

Cap —

Implanted microwire array

Belle in laboratory room in Durham, N.C.

each row represents the activity of a single neuron recorded over time, and each bar indicates that the neuron was firing at a given moment.

The computer, in turn, predicted the trajectory that Belle's arm would take (c) and converted that information into commands for producing the same motion in a robot arm. Then the computer sent commands to a computer that operated a robot arm in a room across the hall. At the same time, it sent commands from our laboratory in Durham, N.C., to another robot in a laboratory hundreds of miles away. In response, both robot arms moved in synchrony with Belle's own limb.   —M. A. L. N. and J. K. C.

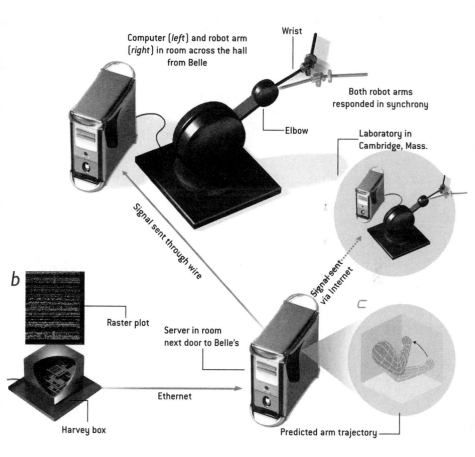

Computer (*left*) and robot arm (*right*) in room across the hall from Belle

Wrist

Both robot arms responded in synchrony

Elbow

Laboratory in Cambridge, Mass.

Signal sent through wire

Signal sent via Internet

b

Raster plot

Server in room next door to Belle's

c

Ethernet

Harvey box

Predicted arm trajectory

There were caveats, however. Georgopoulos had recorded the activity of single neurons one at a time and from only one motor area. This approach left unproved the underlying hypothesis that some kind of coding scheme emerges from the simultaneous activity of many neurons distributed across multiple cortical areas. Scientists knew that the frontal and parietal lobes—in the forward and rear parts of the brain, respectively—interacted to plan and generate motor commands. But technological bottlenecks prevented neurophysiologists from making widespread recordings at once. Furthermore, most scientists believed that by cataloguing the properties of neurons one at a time, they could build a comprehensive map of how the brain works—as if charting the properties of individual trees could unveil the ecological structure of an entire forest!

Fortunately, not everyone agreed. When the two of us met 14 years ago at Hahnemann University, we discussed the challenge of simultaneously recording many single neurons. By 1993 technological breakthroughs we had made allowed us to record 48 neurons spread across five structures that form a rat's sensorimotor system—the brain regions that perceive and use sensory information to direct movements.

Crucial to our success back then—and since—were new electrode arrays containing Teflon-coated stainless-steel microwires that could be implanted in an animal's brain. Neurophysiologists had used standard electrodes that resemble rigid needles to record single neurons. These classic electrodes worked well but only for a few hours, because cellular compounds collected around the electrodes' tips and eventually insulated them from the current. Furthermore, as the subject's brain moved slightly during normal activity, the stiff pins damaged neurons. The microwires we devised in our lab (later produced by NBLabs in Denison, Tex.) had blunter tips, about 50 microns in diameter, and were much more flexible. Cellular substances did not seal off the ends, and the flexibility greatly reduced neuron damage. These properties enabled us to produce recordings for months on end, and having tools for reliable recording allowed us to begin developing systems for translating brain signals into commands that could control a mechanical device.

With electrical engineer Harvey Wiggins, now president of Plexon in Dallas, and with Donald J. Woodward and Samuel A. Deadwyler of Wake Forest University School of Medicine, we devised a small "Harvey box" of custom electronics, like the one next to Belle's booth. It was the first hardware that could properly sample, filter and amplify neural signals from many electrodes. Special software allowed us to discriminate electrical activity from up to four single neurons per microwire by identifying unique features of each cell's electrical discharge.

A Rat's Brain Controls a Lever

IN OUR NEXT EXPERIMENTS at Hahnemann in the mid-1990s, we taught a rat in a cage to control a lever with its mind. First we trained it to press a bar with its forelimb. The bar was electronically connected to a lever outside the cage. When the rat pressed the bar, the outside lever tipped down to a chute and delivered a drop of water it could drink.

We fitted the rat's head with a small version of the brain-machine interface Belle would later use. Every time the rat commanded its forelimb to press the bar, we simultaneously recorded the action potentials produced by 46 neurons. We had programmed resistors in a so-called integrator, which weighted and processed data from the neurons to generate a single analog output that predicted very well the trajectory of the rat's forelimb. We linked this integrator to the robot lever's controller so that it could command the lever.

Once the rat had gotten used to pressing the bar for water, we disconnected the bar from the lever. The rat pressed the bar, but the lever remained still. Frustrated, it began to press the bar repeatedly, to no avail. But one time, the lever tipped and delivered the water. The rat didn't know it, but its 46 neurons had expressed the same firing pattern they had in earlier trials when the bar still worked. That pattern prompted the integrator to put the lever in motion.

After several hours the rat realized it no longer needed to press the bar. If it just looked at the bar and imagined its forelimb pressing it, its neurons could still express the firing pattern that our brain-machine interface would interpret as motor commands to move the lever. Over time, four of six rats succeeded in this task.

They learned that they had to "think through" the motion of pressing the bar. This is not as mystical at it might sound; right now you can imagine reaching out to grasp an object near you—without doing so. In similar fashion, a person with an injured or severed limb might learn to control a robot arm joined to a shoulder.

A Monkey's Brain Controls a Robot Arm

WE WERE THRILLED with our rats' success. It inspired us to move forward, to try to reproduce in a robotic limb the three-dimensional arm movements made by monkeys—animals with brains far more similar to those of humans. As a first step, we had to devise technology for predicting how the monkeys intended to move their natural arms.

At this time, one of us (Nicolelis) moved to Duke and established a neurophysiology laboratory there. Together we built an interface to simultaneously monitor close to 100 neurons, distributed across the frontal and parietal lobes. We proceeded to try it with several owl monkeys. We chose owl monkeys because their motor cortical areas are located on the surface of their smooth brain, a configuration that minimizes the surgical difficulty of implanting microwire arrays. The microwire arrays allowed us to record the action potentials in each creature's brain for several months.

In our first experiments, we required owl monkeys, including Belle, to move a joystick left or right after seeing a light appear on the left or right side of a video screen. We later sat them in a chair facing an opaque barrier. When we lifted the barrier they saw a piece of fruit on a tray. The monkeys had to reach out and grab the fruit, bring it to their mouth and place their hand back down. We measured the position of each monkey's wrist by attaching fiber-optic sensors to it, which defined the wrist's trajectory.

Further analysis revealed that a simple linear summation of the electrical activity of cortical motor neurons predicted very well the position of an animal's hand a few hundred milliseconds ahead of time. This discovery was made by Johan Wessberg of Duke, now at the Gothenburg University in Sweden. The main trick was for the computer to continuously combine neuronal activity produced as far back in time as one second to best predict movements in real time.

As our scientific work proceeded, we acquired a more advanced Harvey box from Plexon. Using it and some custom, real-time algorithms, our computer sampled and integrated the action potentials every 50 to 100 milliseconds. Software translated the output into instructions that could direct the actions of a robot arm in three-dimensional space. Only then did we try to use a BMI to control a robotic device. As we watched our multijointed robot arm accurately mimic Belle's arm movements on that inspiring afternoon in 2000, it was difficult not to ponder the implausibility of it all. Only 50 to 100 neurons randomly sampled from tens of millions were doing the needed work.

Later mathematical analyses revealed that the accuracy of the robot movements was roughly proportional to the number of neurons recorded, but this linear relation began to taper off as the number increased. By sampling 100 neurons we could create robot hand trajectories that were about 70 percent similar to those the monkeys produced. Further analysis estimated that to achieve 95 percent accuracy in the prediction of one-dimensional hand movements, as few as 500 to 700 neurons would suffice, depending on which brain regions we sampled. We are now calculating the number of neurons that would be needed for highly accurate three-dimensional movements. We suspect the total will again be in the hundreds, not thousands.

These results suggest that within each cortical area, the "message" defining a given hand movement is widely disseminated. This decentralization is extremely beneficial to the animal: in case of injury, the animal can fall back on a huge reservoir of redundancy. For us researchers, it means that a BMI neuroprosthesis for severely paralyzed patients may require sampling smaller populations of neurons than was once anticipated.

We continued working with Belle and our other monkeys after Belle's successful experiment. We found that as the animals perfected their tasks, the properties of their neurons changed—over several days or even within a daily two-hour recording session. The contribution of individual neurons varied over time. To cope with this "motor learning," we added a simple routine that enabled our model to reassess periodically the

A Vision of the Future

A BRAIN-MACHINE INTERFACE might someday help a patient whose limbs have been paralyzed by a spine injury. Tiny arrays of microwires implanted in multiple motor cortex areas of the brain would be wired to a neurochip in the skull. As the person imagined her paralyzed arm moving in a particular way, such as reaching out for food on a table, the chip would convert the thoughts into a train of radio-frequency signals and send them wirelessly to a small battery-operated "backpack" computer hanging from the chair.

The computer would convert the signals into motor commands and dispatch them, again wirelessly, to a different chip implanted in the person's arm. This second chip would stimulate nerves needed to move the arm muscles in the desired fashion. Alternatively, the backpack computer could control the wheelchair's motor and steering directly, as the person envisioned where she wanted the chair to roll. Or the computer could send signals to a robotic arm if a natural arm were missing or to a robot arm mounted on a chair. Patrick D. Wolf of Duke University has built a prototype neurochip and backpack, as envisioned here.   —M. A. L. N. and J. K. C.

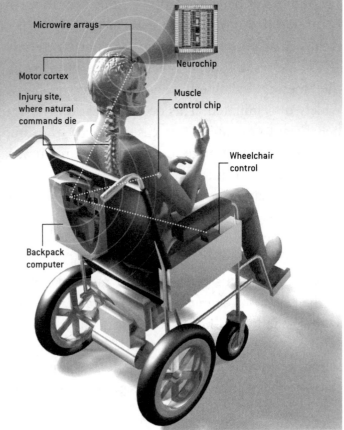

Microwire arrays

Neurochip

Motor cortex

Injury site, where natural commands die

Muscle control chip

Wheelchair control

Backpack computer

contribution of each neuron. Brain cells that ceased to influence the predictions significantly were dropped from the model, and those that became better predictors were added. In essence, we designed a way to extract from the brain a neural output for hand trajectory. This coding, plus our ability to measure neurons reliably over time, allowed our BMI to represent Belle's intended movements accurately for several months. We could have continued, but we had the data we needed.

It is important to note that the gradual changing of neuronal electrical activity helps to give the brain its plasticity. The number of action potentials a neuron generates before a given movement changes as the animal undergoes more experiences. Yet the dynamic revision of neuronal properties does not represent an impediment for practical BMIs. The beauty of a distributed neural output is that it does not rely on a small group of neurons. If a BMI can maintain viable recordings from hundreds to thousands of single neurons for months to years and utilize models that can learn, it can handle evolving neurons, neuronal death and even degradation in electrode-recording capabilities.

Exploiting Sensory Feedback

BELLE PROVED THAT A BMI can work for a primate brain. But could we adapt the interface to more complex brains? In May 2001 we began studies with three macaque monkeys at Duke. Their brains contain deep furrows and convolutions that resemble those of the human brain.

We employed the same BMI used for Belle, with one fundamental addition: now the monkeys could exploit visual feedback to judge for themselves how well the BMI could mimic their hand movements. We let the macaques move a joystick in random directions, driving a cursor across a computer screen. Suddenly a round target would appear somewhere on the screen. To receive a sip of fruit juice, the monkey had to position the cursor quickly inside the target—within 0.5 second—by rapidly manipulating the joystick.

The first macaque to master this task was Aurora, an elegant female who clearly enjoyed showing off that she could hit the target more than 90 percent of the time. For a year, our postdoctoral fellows Roy Crist and José Carmena recorded the activity of up to 92 neurons in five frontal and parietal areas of Aurora's cortex.

Once Aurora commanded the game, we started playing a trick on her. In about 30 percent of the trials we disabled the connection between the joystick and the cursor. To move the cursor quickly within the target, Aurora had to rely solely on her brain activity, processed by our BMI. After being puzzled, Aurora gradually altered her strategy. Although she continued to make hand movements, after a few days she learned she could control the cursor 100 percent of the time with her brain alone. In a few trials each day during the ensuing weeks Aurora didn't even bother to move her hand; she moved the cursor by just thinking about the trajectory it should take.

That was not all. Because Aurora could see her performance on the screen, the BMI made better and better predictions even though it was recording the same neurons. Although much more analysis is required to understand this result, one explanation is that the visual feedback helped Aurora to maximize the BMI's reaction to both brain and machine learning. If this proves true, visual or other sensory feedback could allow people to improve the performance of their own BMIs.

We observed another encouraging result. At this writing, it has been a year since we implanted the microwires in Aurora's brain, and we continue to record 60 to 70 neurons daily. This extended success indicates that even in a primate with a convoluted brain, our microwire arrays can provide long-term, high-quality, multichannel signals. Although this sample is down from the original 92 neurons, Aurora's performance with the BMI remains at the highest levels she has achieved.

We will make Aurora's tasks more challenging. In May we began modifying the BMI to give her tactile feedback for new experiments that are now beginning. The BMI will control a nearby robot arm fitted with a gripper that simulates a grasping hand. Force sensors will indicate when the gripper encounters an object and how much force is required to hold it. Tactile feedback—is the object heavy or light, slick or sticky?—will be delivered to a patch on Aurora's skin embedded with small vibrators. Variations in the vibration frequencies should help Aurora figure out how much force the robot arm should apply to, say, pick up a piece of fruit, and to hold it as the robot brings it back to her. This experiment might give us the most concrete evidence yet that a person suffering from severe paralysis could regain basic arm movements through an implant in the brain that communicated over wires, or wirelessly, with signal generators embedded in a limb.

If visual and tactile sensations mimic the information that usually flows between Aurora's own arm and brain, long-term interaction with a BMI could possibly stimulate her brain to incorporate the robot into its representations of her body—schema known to exist in most brain regions. In other words, Aurora's brain might represent this artificial device as another part of her body. Neuronal tissue in her brain might even dedicate itself to operating the robot arm and interpreting its feedback.

To test whether this hypothesis has merit, we plan to conduct experiments like those done with Aurora, except that an animal's arm will be temporarily anesthetized, thereby removing any natural feedback information. We predict that after a transition period, the primate will be able to interact with the BMI just fine. If the animal's brain does meld the robot arm into its body representations, it is reasonable to expect that a paraplegic's brain would do the same, rededicating neurons that once served a natural limb to the operation of an artificial one.

Each advance shows how plastic the brain is. Yet there will always be limits. It is unlikely, for example,

Stopping Seizures

RECENT EXPERIMENTS SUGGEST that brain-machine interfaces could one day help prevent brain seizures in people who suffer from severe chronic epilepsy, which causes dozens of seizures a day. The condition ruins a patient's quality of life and can lead to permanent brain damage. To make matters worse, patients usually become unresponsive to traditional drug therapy.

A BMI for seizure control would function somewhat like a heart pacemaker. It would continuously monitor the brain's electrical activity for patterns that indicate an imminent attack. If the BMI sensed such a pattern, it would deliver an electrical stimulus to the brain or a peripheral nerve that would quench the rising storm or trigger the release of antiepileptic medication.

At Duke we demonstrated the feasibility of this concept in collaboration with Erika E. Fanselow, now at Brown University, and Ashlan P. Reid, now at the University of Pennsylvania. We implanted a BMI with arrays of microwires in rats given PTZ, a drug that induces repetitive mild epilepsy. When a seizure starts, cortical neurons begin firing together in highly synchronized bursts. When the "brain pacemaker" detected this pattern, it triggered the electrical stimulation of the large trigeminal cranial nerve. The brief stimulus disrupted the epileptic activity quickly and efficiently, without damaging the nerve, and reduced the occurrence and duration of seizures.
—M. A. L. N. and J. K. C.

that a stroke victim could gain full control over a robot limb. Stroke damage is usually widespread and involves so much of the brain's white matter—the fibers that allow brain regions to communicate—that the destruction overwhelms the brain's plastic capabilities. This is why stroke victims who lose control of uninjured limbs rarely regain it.

Reality Check

GOOD NEWS NOTWITHSTANDING, we researchers must be very cautious about offering false hope to people with serious disabilities. We must still overcome many hurdles before BMIs can be considered safe, reliable and efficient therapeutic options. We have to demonstrate in clinical trials that a proposed BMI will offer much greater well-being while posing no risk of added neurological damage.

Surgical implantation of electrode arrays will always be of medical concern, for instance. Investigators need to evaluate whether highly dense microwire arrays can provide viable recordings without causing tissue damage or infection in humans. Progress toward dense arrays is already under way. Duke electronics technician Gary Lehew has designed ways to increase significantly the number of microwires mounted in an array that is light and easy to implant. We can now implant multiple arrays, each of which has up to 160 microwires and measures five by eight millimeters, smaller than a pinky fingernail. We recently implanted 704 microwires across eight cortical areas in a macaque and recorded 318 neurons simultaneously.

In addition, considerable miniaturization of electronics and batteries must occur. We have begun collaborating with José Carlos Príncipe of the University of Florida to craft implantable microelectronics that will embed in hardware the neuronal pattern recognition we now do with software, thereby eventually freeing the BMI from a computer. These microchips will thus have to send wireless control data to robotic actuators. Working with Patrick D. Wolf's lab at Duke, we have built the first wireless "neurochip" and beta-tested it with Aurora. Seeing streams of neural activity flash on a laptop many meters away from Aurora—broadcast via the first wireless connection between a primate's brain and a computer—was a delight.

More and more scientists are embracing the vision that BMIs can help people in need. In the past year, several traditional neurological laboratories have begun to pursue neuroprosthetic devices. Preliminary results from Arizona State University, Brown University and the California Institute of Technology have recently appeared. Some of the studies provide independent confirmation of the rat and monkey studies we have done. Researchers at Arizona State basically reproduced our 3-D approach in owl monkeys and showed that it can work in rhesus monkeys too. Scientists at Brown enabled a rhesus macaque monkey to move a cursor around a computer screen. Both groups recorded 10 to 20 neurons or so per animal. Their success further demonstrates that this new field is progressing nicely.

The most useful BMIs will exploit hundreds to a few thousand single neurons distributed over multiple motor regions in the frontal and parietal lobes. Those that record only a small number of neurons (say, 30 or fewer) from a single cortical area would never provide clinical help, because they would lack the excess capacity required to adapt to neuronal loss or changes in neuronal responsiveness. The other extreme—recording millions of neurons using large electrodes—would most likely not work either, because it might be too invasive.

Noninvasive methods, though promising for some therapies, will probably be of limited use for controlling prostheses with thoughts. Scalp recording, called electroencephalography (EEG), is a noninvasive technique that can drive a different kind of brain-machine interface, however. Niels Birbaumer of the University of Tübingen in Germany has successfully used EEG recordings and a computer interface to help patients paralyzed by severe neurological disorders learn how to modulate their EEG activity to select letters on a computer screen, so they can write messages. The process is time-consuming but offers the only way for these people to communicate with the world. Yet EEG signals cannot be used directly for limb prostheses, because they depict the average electrical activity of broad populations of neurons; it is difficult to extract from them the fine variations needed to encode precise arm and hand movements.

Despite the remaining hurdles, we have plenty of reasons to be optimistic. Although it may be a decade before we witness the operation of the first human neuroprosthesis, all the amazing possibilities crossed our minds that afternoon in Durham as we watched the activity of Belle's neurons flashing on a computer monitor. We will always remember our sense of awe as we eavesdropped on the processes by which the primate brain generates a thought. Belle's thought to receive her juice was a simple one, but a thought it was, and it commanded the outside world to achieve her very real goal.

More To Explore

Real-Time Control of a Robot Arm Using Simultaneously Recorded Neurons in the Motor Cortex. J. K. Chapin, K. A. Moxon, R. S. Markowitz and M.A.L. Nicolelis in *Nature Neurosciences*, Vol. 2, pages 664–670; July 1999.

Real-Time Prediction of Hand Trajectory by Ensembles of Cortical Neurons in Primates. J. Wessberg, C. R. Stambaugh, J. D. Kralik, P. D. Beck, J. K. Chapin, J. Kim, S. J. Biggs, M. A. Srinivasan and M.A.L. Nicolelis in *Nature*, Vol. 408, pages 361–365; November 16, 2000.

Actions from Thoughts. M.A.L. Nicolelis in *Nature*, Vol. 409, pages 403–407; January 18, 2001.

Advances in Neural Population Coding. Edited by M.A.L. Nicolelis. Progress in Brain Research, Vol. 130. Elsevier, 2001.

Neural Prostheses for Restoration of Sensory and Motor Function. Edited by J. K. Chapin and K. A. Moxon. CRC Press, 2001.

The Authors

MIGUEL A. L. NICOLELIS and *JOHN K. CHAPIN* have collaborated for more than a decade. Nicolelis, a native of Brazil, received his M.D. and Ph.D. in neurophysiology from the University of São Paulo. After postdoctoral work at Hahnemann University, he joined Duke University, where he now co-directs the Center for Neuroengineering and is professor of neurobiology, biomedical engineering, and psychological and brain sciences. Chapin received his Ph.D. in neurophysiology from the University of Rochester and has held faculty positions at the University of Texas and the MCP Hahnemann University School of Medicine (now Drexel University College of Medicine). He is currently professor of physiology and pharmacology at the State University of New York Downstate Medical Center.

"An Army of
4. Small Robots"

by Robert Grabowski, Luis E. Navarro-Serment,
and Pradeep K. Khosla

For robot designers these days, small is beautiful

A group of terrorists has stormed into an office
building and taken an unknown number of people
hostage. They have blocked the entrances and covered
the windows. No one outside can see how many they
are, what weapons they carry or where they are holding
their hostages. But suddenly a SWAT team bursts into
the room and captures the assailants before they can
even grab their weapons. How did the commandos get
the information they needed to move so confidently
and decisively?

The answer is a team of small, coordinated robots.
They infiltrated the building through the ventilation
system and methodically moved throughout the ducts.
Some were equipped with microphones to monitor
conversations, others with small video cameras, still
others with sensors that sniffed the air for chemical or
biological agents. Working together, they radioed this
real-time information back to the authorities.

This is roughly the scenario that the Defense
Advanced Research Projects Agency (DARPA) presented
to robotics researchers in 1998. Their challenge was to
develop tiny reconnaissance robots that soldiers could

carry on their backs and scatter on the floor like popcorn. On the home front, firefighters and search-and-rescue workers could toss these robots through windows and let them scoot around to look for trapped victims or sniff out toxic materials. For now, these scenarios—let alone the lifelike robots depicted in science-fiction movies such as *Minority Report*—remain well beyond the state of the art. Yet the vision of mini robots has captured the attention of leading robot designers. Rather than concentrate on a few large platforms bristling with sensors (like Swiss Army knives on wheels), the focus these days is shifting toward building fleets of small, light and simple robots.

In principle, lilliputian robots have numerous advantages over their bulkier cousins. They can crawl through pipes, inspect collapsed buildings and hide in inconspicuous niches. A well-organized group of them can exchange sensor information to map objects that cannot be easily comprehended from a single vantage point. They can come to the aid of one another to scale obstacles or recover from a fall. Depending on the situation, the team leader can send in a bigger or smaller number of robots. If one robot fails, the entire mission is not lost; the rest can carry on.

But diminutive robots require a new design philosophy. They do not have the luxury of abundant power and space, as do their larger cousins, and they cannot house all the components necessary to execute a given mission. Even carrying something as compact as a video camera can nearly overwhelm a little robot.

Consequently, their sensors, processing power and
physical strength must be distributed among several
robots, which must then work in unison. Such robots
are like ants in a colony: weak and vulnerable on their
own but highly effective when they join forces.

Whegs, Golf Balls and Tin Cans

RESEARCHERS HAVE TAKEN various approaches to the
problems of building robots at this scale. Some have
adopted a biological approach to mimic the attributes
of insects and animals. For example, robot designers
at Case Western Reserve University have developed a
highly mobile platform modeled after a cockroach. It
uses a hybrid of wheels and legs ("whegs") to scoot
across uneven terrain. A team from the University of
Michigan at Ann Arbor has come up with a two-legged
robot with suction cups at the ends of its articulated
limbs that allow it to climb walls, much like a caterpillar.

Biology has inspired not only the physical shape of
the robots but also their control systems. Roboticists
at the Massachusetts Institute of Technology have
invented robots the size of golf balls that forage for
food in the same fashion as ants. They use simple light
sensors to express "emotions" to one another and to
make decisions collectively. This type of research
takes its cue from the work of famous robot scientist
Rodney A. Brooks. In the behavior-based control
algorithms that he pioneered, each robot reacts to
local stimuli. There is no central plan, no colonel

commanding the troops. Instead the team's action emerges as a consequence of the combination of individuals interacting with one another. As innovative as this approach is, many problems remain before it can bear fruit. Deliberate missions require deliberate actions and deliberate plans—something that emergent behavior cannot reliably provide, at least not yet.

On the more deliberate side, researchers at the University of Minnesota have developed scouts, robots that can be launched like grenades through windows. Shaped like tin cans, these two-wheeled devices are equipped with video cameras that allow them to be teleoperated by a controlling user. Similarly, PARC (formerly known as Xerox PARC) in Palo Alto, Calif., has created a highly articulated snake robot that can be guided via remote video by a user. It literally crawls over obstacles and through pipes. Like the scouts, though, these robots currently lack sufficient local sensing and must rely on a human operator for decision making. This handicap currently makes them unwieldy for deployment in large numbers.

A few small robot platforms have become commercially available over the past few years.

Overview/Millibots

- Small robots will one day complement their larger, pricier cousins. Bots the size of Matchbox cars could scurry down pipes and crawl through the debris of collapsed buildings—very useful skills in espionage, surveillance, and search and rescue.
- Limited by size and battery power, small robots do not have the capabilities of a single larger robot. They must divvy up tasks and work together as a team, which is not as easy as it might sound. Engineers have had to develop new techniques for tasks such as ascertaining position and mapping territory.

Khepera, a hockey-puck-size robot developed in Switzerland, has become popular among researchers interested in behavior-based control. Hobbyists, too, are experimenting with the technology. Living Machines in Lompoc, Calif., puts out a tiny programmable robot known as Pocket-Bot. Along the same lines, Lego Mindstorms, an extension to the popular Lego toy bricks, allows the general public to build and operate simple robots. Already they are being used in science projects and college contests. But the sensing and control for these commercial designs remain extremely rudimentary, and they lack the competence for complex missions.

Power Shortage

HERE AT CARNEGIE MELLON UNIVERSITY, the emphasis is on flexibility. We have built a team of about a dozen "millibots," each about five centimeters on a side. This is the scale at which we could still use off-the-shelf components for sensing and processing, although we had to custom-design the circuit boards and controllers. Each robot consists of three main modules: one for mobility, one for control and one for sensing. The mobility module sits on the bottom. Its two motors drive treads made from small O-rings. The present version can move across office floors and rugs at a maximum speed of about 20 centimeters a second, or about a sixth of normal human walking speed. As we develop new mobility platforms, we can snap them into place without having to redesign the rest of the robot.

Anatomy Of A Millibot

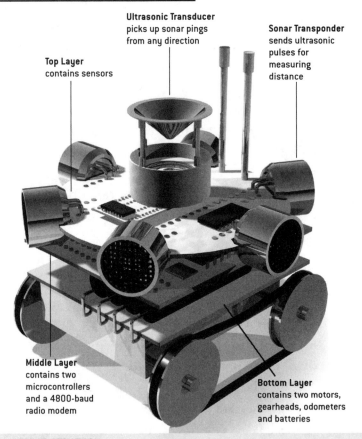

Ultrasonic Transducer
picks up sonar pings
from any direction

Sonar Transponder
sends ultrasonic
pulses for
measuring
distance

Top Layer
contains sensors

Middle Layer
contains two
microcontrollers
and a 4800-baud
radio modem

Bottom Layer
contains two motors,
gearheads, odometers
and batteries

MAPPING STRATEGY

By using one another as reference points, millibots can find their way through an
unknown space. In this example, three robots fix themselves in place and act as beacons.
The fourth robot surveys the area using its sonar. When it is done, the robots
switch roles. The lead robots become the new beacons, and the rearmost millibot
begins moving around and taking data. The maps thus collected can be stitched
together into a larger composite map of the entire area.

LOCALIZATION

One robot simultaneously sends out an ultrasonic and radio pulse. The others receive the radio pulse instantaneously and the sound pulse shortly after. The time difference is a measure of the distance.

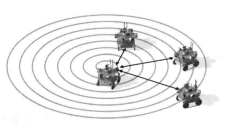

The robots take turns sending and receiving pulses.

A computer uses the distance measurements to deduce the position of each robot. One caveat is that mirror-image arrangements give the same set of measurements.

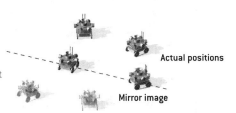

Actual positions

Mirror image

This ambiguity is resolved by having one of the robots take a left turn and measuring its new position, which will differ depending on which mirror image is the correct arrangement.

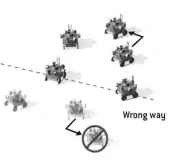

Wrong way

Millibot Chain

DURING NORMAL OPERATION, individual millibots explore their space and share information to build maps. When the team reaches an impasse, such as a ledge or a flight of stairs, they come together to form an articulated train.

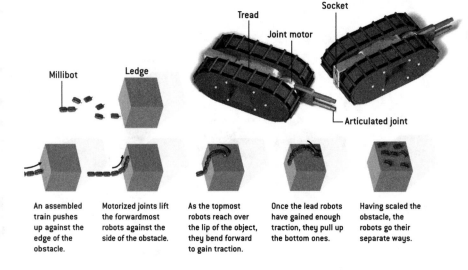

An assembled train pushes up against the edge of the obstacle.

Motorized joints lift the forwardmost robots against the side of the obstacle.

As the topmost robots reach over the lip of the object, they bend forward to gain traction.

Once the lead robots have gained enough traction, they pull up the bottom ones.

Having scaled the obstacle, the robots go their separate ways.

The middle module provides processing and control. The current design contains an eight-bit microcontroller akin to the ones used in personal computers of the early 1980s. Though no match for modern desktop computers, these processors can still perform real-time control for the robot. The sensing module, which sits on top, includes sonar and near-infrared sensors for measuring the distance to nearby obstacles; a mid-infrared sensor (like those used in motion detectors) for detecting warm bodies; a video camera for surveillance; and a radio modem for communicating with other robots or the home base.

Perhaps the most severe limitation on these and other small robots is power. Batteries are bulky and heavy. They do not scale well: as its size is reduced, a battery reaches a threshold at which it cannot supply the power needed to move its own weight. The two rechargeable NiMH cellular-phone batteries on our millibots take up about a third of the available space. They provide enough power for only a limited array of sensors and a run time of between 30 and 90 minutes, depending on the complexity of the mission. Larger batteries would increase the run time but crowd out necessary components. Small-robot design is all about compromise. Speed, duration and functionality compete with weight, size and component availability.

To deal with these constraints, we have adopted two design methodologies for the millibots: specialization and collaboration. The former means that a robot is equipped with only enough sensing and processing for a specific task, allowing it to make optimal use of the available room and power. In a typical mission, some millibots are charged with making maps of the surroundings. Others provide live feedback for the human operator or carry sensors specific to that mission. To get the job done, the robots must collaborate.

Where Are We?

ONE VITAL TASK that requires collaboration is localization: figuring out the team's position. Larger robots have the luxury of several techniques to ascertain their position, such as Global Positioning System (GPS) receivers, fixed beacons and visual landmark recognition. Moreover, they have the processing power to match current sensor information to existing maps.

None of these techniques works reliably for midget robots. They have a limited sensor range; the millibot sonar can measure distances out to about two meters. They are too small to carry GPS units. Dead reckoning—the technique of tracking position by measuring the wheel speed—is frustrated by their low weight. Something as seemingly inconsequential as the direction of the weave of a rug can dramatically influence their motion, making odometry readings inaccurate, just as a car's odometer would fail to give accurate distances if driven on an ice-covered lake.

So we have had to come up with a new technique. What we have developed is a miniaturized version of GPS. Rather than satellites, this technique utilizes sound waves to measure the distances between robots in the group. Each millibot is equipped with an ultrasonic transducer in addition to its radio modem. To determine distance, a millibot simultaneously emits a radio pulse and an ultrasonic signal, which radiate in all directions. The other robots listen for the two signals. The radio wave, traveling at the speed of light, arrives essentially instantaneously. The sound, moving at roughly 340 meters a second, arrives a few milliseconds later, depending on the distance between the robot sending the signal and the robot receiving it. A cone-shaped piece of metal on the sensing module reflects ultrasound down onto a transducer, allowing the robots to detect sound from any direction. The process is analogous to measuring the distance to an approaching storm by timing the interval between lightning and thunder.

By alternating their transmitting and listening roles, the robots figure out the distances between them. Each measurement takes about 30 milliseconds to complete. The team leader—either the home base or a larger robot, perhaps the mother bot that deployed the millibots—collects all the information and calculates robot positions using trilateration. Trilateration resembles the better-known technique of triangulation, except that it relies on distances rather than compass headings to get a fix on position. In two dimensions, each range estimate indicates that another robot lies somewhere on a circle around the transmitting robot. The intersection of two or more circles marks the potential location of other robots [*see box on page 63*]. The algorithm finds the arrangement of robots that best satisfies all the circle intersections and range measurements.

One thing that complicates the procedure is that more than one arrangement of robots may match the data. Another is that range measurements are prone to error and uncertainty. Ultrasonic signals echo off floors and walls, creating ambiguity in the distance readings. In fact, depending on the geometry, wave interference can cause the signal to vanish altogether. For this reason, we developed an algorithm that combines the ultrasonic ranging with dead reckoning, which, despite its problems, provides enough additional information to resolve the ambiguities. The algorithm estimates the measurement error and computes the set of robot positions that minimizes the overall error.

The advantage of this localization method is that the millibots do not need fixed reference points to navigate. They can enter an unfamiliar space and survey it on their own. During mapping, a few selected millibots serve as beacons. These robots remain stationary while the others move around, mapping and avoiding objects while measuring their position relative to the beacons. When the team has fully explored the area around the beacons, the robots switch roles. The exploring robots position themselves as beacons, and the previous set begins to explore. This technique is similar to the children's game of leapfrog, and it can be executed without human intervention.

Chain of Command

OBSTACLES PRESENT small robots with another reason to collaborate. By virtue of its size, a little robot is susceptible to the random clutter that pervades our lives. It must deal with rocks, dirt and loose paper. The standard millibot has a clearance of about 15 millimeters, so a pencil or twig can stop it in its tracks. To get around these limitations, we have come up with a newer version of the millibots that can couple together like train cars. Each of these new millibots, about 11 centimeters long and six centimeters wide, looks like a miniature World War I–style tank. Typically they roam around independently and are versatile enough to get over small obstacles. But when they need to cross a ditch or scale a flight of stairs, they can link up to form a chain.

What gives the chain its versatility is the coupling joint between millibots. Unlike a train couple or a trailer hitch on a car, the millibot coupling joint contains a powerful motor that can rotate the joint up or down with enough torque to lift several millibots. To climb a stair, the chain first pushes up against the base of the stair. One of the millibots near the center of the chain then cantilevers up the front part of chain. Those millibots that reach the top can then pull up the lower ones [*see illustration on page 64*]. Right now this process has to be remotely controlled by humans, but eventually the chain should be able to scale stairs automatically.

Already researchers' attention has begun to turn from hardware development toward the design of better control systems. The emphasis will shift from the control of a few individuals to the management of hundreds or thousands—a fundamentally different challenge that will require expertise from related fields such as economics, military logistics and even political science.

One of the ways we envision large-scale control is through hierarchy. Much like the military, robots will be divided into smaller teams controlled by a local leader. This leader will be responsible to a higher authority. Already millibots are being directed by larger, tanklike robots whose Pentium processors can handle the complex calculations of mapping and localization. These larger robots can tow a string of millibots behind them like ducklings and, when necessary, deploy them in an area of interest. They themselves report to larger all-terrain-vehicle robots in our group, which have multiple computers, video cameras, GPS units and a range of a few hundred kilometers. The idea is that the larger robots will deploy the smaller ones in areas that they cannot access themselves and then remain nearby to provide support and direction.

To be sure, small robots have a long way to go. Outside of a few laboratories, no small-robot teams are roaming the halls of buildings searching for danger. Although the potential of these robots remains vast, their current capabilities place them just above novelty— which is about where mobile phones and handheld computers were a decade ago. As the technology filters down from the military applications and others, we expect the competence of the small robot to improve significantly. Working as teams, they have a full repertoire of skills; their modular design allows them to be customized to particular missions; and, not least, they are fun to work with.

More To Explore

Behavior-Based Robotics (Intelligent Robotics and Autonomous Agents). Ronald C. Arkin. MIT Press, 1998.

Heterogeneous Teams of Modular Robots for Mapping, and Exploration. Robert Grabowski, Luis Navarro-Serment, Christopher J. J. Paredis and Pradeep K. Khosla in special issue on heterogeneous multi-robot systems, *Autonomous Robots*, Vol. 8, No. 3, pages 293–308; June 2000.

Millibot Trains for Enhanced Mobility. H. Benjamin Brown, J. Michael Vande Weghe, Curt A. Bererton and Pradeep K. Khosla in *IEEE/ASME Transactions on Mechatronics*, Vol. 7, No. 4, pages 452–461; December 2002.

For more information and links to various projects: **www.andrew.cmu.edu/~rjg/army.html**

The Author

ROBERT GRABOWSKI, LUIS E. NAVARRO-SERMENT and *PRADEEP K. KHOSLA* began working together on the millibot project in the summer of 1999. Khosla is chair of the electrical and computer engineering department at Carnegie Mellon University. He made his name in robotics by developing the first direct-drive manipulator arms, which are now used in most automated factories. Grabowski and Navarro-Serment are Ph.D. students. Grabowski served eight years in the U.S. Navy working with nuclear reactors. He has tinkered with electronics all his life and still enjoys playing with Legos and taking apart old VCRs. Navarro-Serment's background is in industrial automa-tion and control systems; he used to head the electrical engineering department of the Guadalajara campus of the Monterrey Institute of Technology and Higher Education in Mexico. He is an avid amateur astronomer. The authors thank the rest of the millibot team—Chris Paredis, Ben Brown, Curt Bererton and Mike Vande Weghe—for their invaluable contributions.

"Plug-and-Play
5. Robots"

by W. Wayt Gibbs

*Personal robots may soon be as cheap
and customizable as personal computers*

"Could this be the place?" I wonder as I stand before
a nondescript storefront, formerly a tattoo parlor, in
the tiny borough of Youngwood, Pa. The windows are
covered by blinds; the door bears forbidding bars. The
building lacks a sign or even a house number. It seems
an odd location from which to launch an ambitious
new species of robot.

But when Thomas J. Burick opens the door and I
see three prototype "PC-Bots" sitting on his small
workbench, I realize that this 34-year-old entrepreneur
is no ordinary inventor. The half-meter-high robots
look like R2-D2 droids that have been redesigned by
Cadillac. Burick says that he spent a year honing their
appearance, something almost unheard of in serious
robotics, where function usually trumps form.

To Burick, form is function, and it is very important
that he get the design right the first time. This is his
life's dream, and it has consumed his life savings. "As
a kid, I watched *Lost in Space* on TV and thought it
was so fantastic that Will Robinson had this machine
who protected him and was the best friend anyone could
have," he says, with boyish earnestness. In seventh

grade Burick built a voice-controlled mobile robot, and in high school he constructed an autonomous fire-fighting rover.

As he got older, Burick dabbled with the low-level microcontrollers, servos and sensors used these days by amateur robot builders, but he finally gave up in frustration. His jobs had been in retail, selling consumer electronics rather than making them. With no formal training in programming or electrical engineering, "the learning curve was too steep," he says. "I thought there has got to be a better way."

The better way occurred to him 18 months ago as he was repairing one of the generic "white box" PCs he assembles from components and sells at his small computer store half a block up the street. What if robots could be built up from interchangeable, commodity parts just the way that desktop computers are? Better yet, what if there were a robotic platform that could accept the thousands of plug-and-play PC peripherals and accessories already on the market?

Soon there will be. White Box Robotics, Burick's nascent company, is preparing three varieties of its mobile robotic chassis for mass production this summer. Sitting on the workbench, each of the final prototypes for the three robots looks quite distinct.

"This one is customized for security," Burick says, putting his hand on the 912 HMV. "It's painted with the same paint used on the Hummer H2," he notes. Hella driving lamps are mounted on its front, and webcams peer out from its head and belly. "It could patrol your house while you are away and e-mail or page you if it detects a loud noise or an unfamiliar person."

"And we call this one the 912 MP3," Burick says, gesturing toward a white robot of the same size and shape but sporting a color LCD screen in its back, a stereo control panel in its midriff and a striking blue lamp in its head instead of a camera. "We designed this to appeal to young people, who could use it as their bedroom computer. It can download music and play DVDs in response to voice commands."

But at the moment it is the third robot, the basic model, that illustrates Burick's idea best. Its exterior shell has been removed to reveal an inner skeleton, common to all three siblings, that allows them to work like PCs on wheels.

A simple metal frame holds up to six shelves at various positions. "All of the electronics mount on these trays, which slide out," he explains. One tray holds the motherboard, which is a diminutive Mini-ITX made by VIA that crams an Intel-compatible processor with 512 megabytes of memory, video, audio and networking chips all onto a circuit board the size of a bread plate. Another tray contains two hefty but inexpensive 12-volt batteries that allow the robot to run for three hours between charges. Standard laptop hard drives, CD burners, DVD drives—virtually any PC gadget you can find at CompUSA—can be mounted securely to these trays inside the robot's body.

"These robots run Windows XP, so they can do anything your PC will do," Burick points out. But they can also do things that no PC can—move, for example. Below the metal frame is a drive assembly: two motors connected to two four-inch wheels and a spring-mounted hard plastic ball. "This Delrin ball keeps the robot stable even on uneven surfaces and allows it to track its position precisely even as it turns and spins," he notes. "And this whole drive assembly comes off with four bolts, so if you want to replace it—with tank-style treads, for example—it's a five-minute job." Eventually he hopes to offer an optional drive mechanism capable of climbing stairs.

With an oomph, Burick lifts the 40-pound machine down to the floor and turns it on. To my surprise, the 18-inch-tall rover is quieter than my laptop computer. Just like any PC, it has ports on its backside for a monitor, keyboard, mouse, Ethernet cable and so on. But untethering the machine is only a matter of plugging an inexpensive WiFi receiver into the motherboard. Burick uses his laptop to log in over the wireless link. "Okay, this software is now running on the robot," he says as he launches the Robot Control Center, a program he has licensed from Evolution Robotics.

Clicking on buttons in the program, he drives the robot toward a 20-year-old Heath Hero Junior robot gathering dust in the corner. When it gets within three feet or so, the 912 stops and says in its synthesized voice, "Hello, Hero Junior."

It's a nice trick, and as I try the software myself, I find that creating such pseudointelligent behaviors is quite simple. A small window shows onscreen what the robot sees through its "eye" camera. Burick sets a model of the B9 robot from *Lost in Space* on the floor, and I turn the 912 to look at it. I click the "capture" button, and the machine adds it to a memorized list of objects that it can recognize. I back the 912 up, turn it around, and create a new behavior by checking a box here and making a menu selection there. Six clicks later I have taught it to speak a phrase whenever it sees the B9 toy. And it works: even from four feet away and at an odd angle, the 912 recognizes the toy and says, "Hey, get out of my way!"

It is a trivial example of a powerful combination: easy-to-use software and easily customized hardware. Plug in a microphone, and the robot can respond to voice commands. Attach an infrared sensor and tuck a few speakers in its case, and it becomes a CD player that follows you around the house. Bolt on a couple of gripper arms, and you can program it to empty the kitty litter box every other day.

Because the chassis can be stamped out by the same factories that make computer cases, the PC-Bots will cost in the neighborhood of $1,000—about as much as a decent desktop system, Burick declares: "My goal is to make it affordable enough that a 14-year-old can buy one with the money earned on a paper route. I want people to use this platform like a blank canvas, to let their imaginations run wild."

6. "Robots That Suck"

by George Musser

Have they finally come out with a robot for the rest of us?

For generations, tinkerers have been pointing out how much their projects will lighten the load of housework. For generations, spouses and parents have failed to be impressed by these claims. When I built my first robot seven years ago, people kept asking, "So what does it do?" I explained that it would eventually vacuum the floor. I should have just been honest: "Not much, but it sure is cool, isn't it?" All these years later I still have trouble getting my creations to do the most basic things, like move in a straight line. My professions of usefulness don't carry much weight around the house anymore.

At least I am not alone. Seldom in the history of technology has an industry been so eagerly anticipated, and so slow to emerge, as the consumer robot industry. Back in the early 1980s, when computers were turning from hobbyist playthings into mass-market appliances, it looked as though robots would soon follow. Heathkit's famous Hero I robot kit came out in 1982, not long after the original IBM PC. *Entrepreneur* magazine predicted a $2-billion home robot market by 1990. Today the original PC is a museum piece, and Hero I is still the state of the art.

Anyone who builds a robot appreciates what happened. When humans use a personal computer, we enter into the computer's world. If it can't do something, or if it crashes, too bad; we have to deal. But a robot enters into our world. If floors are uneven, if legs get in the way, if lighting conditions change, the robot has to deal. Extra computing power doesn't necessarily help; on the contrary, more sophistication typically means less resilience.

Through the school of hard knocks (lots of them), robot experimenters have learned to keep things simple. Massachusetts Institute of Technology professor and robo-guru Rodney A. Brooks led the way in the mid-1980s with a new style of robot programming, in which cheap sensors directly trigger elementary behaviors. Most robot kits these days, such as Lego Mindstorms, embrace this approach. And a similar design philosophy is reviving the fortunes of the home robot industry.

Some products, admittedly, achieve simplicity by giving up the pretense of doing anything useful at all. Robot dogs such as Sony's Aibo are the classic example. Others, such as robotic lawnmowers and pool cleaners, aim to do a single task in a highly controlled environment. The next step up is to do a single task in a highly uncontrolled environment, and the most obvious candidate for that is vacuuming. Over the past several years, a number of companies have promised to roll out floor-cleaning robots. A few of them have even delivered.

Apart from DustBot, a cheap but clever toy made by the Japanese company Tomy, the first consumer robot that could vacuum was Cye. Released in 1999 by Pittsburgh-based Probotics, Cye is the Apple II of robots: just pull it out of the box and plug it in. I tested one back in the fall of 2000. It's about the size of a toaster oven, with two wheels, a pair of wheel odometers to measure its movement, and a bump switch to sense when it hits something. To prove its usefulness, it can tow a small upright vacuum cleaner.

You control Cye from a PC via a wireless link, and the desktop software is where Cye really shines. As the bot blunders around, it relays back odometry readings, and the software estimates its position by dead reckoning. Crucially, the software keeps track of the uncertainty in its position; periodically the robot can reduce the error by reorienting against an object of known position, such as a wall. You can map a room, automatically calculate paths from A to B, and designate no-Cye zones—very handy in a home or office where not everyone shares your robotic enthusiasm.

For all its dummy-proofing, though, Cye still appeals mainly to gadget freaks. The price, which used to be $700 until the company lost its senses and raised it to $2,700, puts off the practical-minded. The mapping software tends to crash, and the vacuuming mode is primitive—the bot sweeps back and forth in a rectan-gular area and doesn't suffer obstacles gladly. Even I got bored. Lacking other sensors or the provision to run your own programs, Cye isn't capable of the richness of behavior that even entry-level kits can provide.

Last October, Brooks's own firm, iRobot, based in Somerville, Mass., brought out Roomba, a robot tailor-made for vacuuming. The lead designer, Joseph L. Jones, is co-author of the 1993 book *Mobile Robots: Inspiration to Implementation*, which remains the single best guide for beginning hobbyists (it got me started). The main subject of the book, the Rug Warrior project, grew out of a floor-cleaning bot that Jones had built for a contest at M.I.T. Four years ago he and mechanical engineer Paul Sandin finally got company backing to turn it into a product.

Roomba is roughly the size of a car hubcap and weighs about six pounds. The main cleaning mechanism is basically a Bissell carpet sweeper—one of those rug cleaners that is often found (and sometimes used) in college dorm rooms. A zigzagging wire forms a cage to keep the rotating brush from choking on the corners of rugs. A miniature weed whacker on the side flicks dust away from the base of walls. Behind the sweeper are two squeegee blades with a narrow slot between them—a "microvacuum" designed to suck up dust and hair. (Jones says the battery couldn't power a full-size vacuum.) The dirt ends up in a plastic cartridge.

The only controls are an "on" switch and three buttons to specify whether the room is small, medium or large. When you press one, Roomba starts moving in a spiral; after a while, it goes straight until it hits something, then turns, sometimes heading back toward the center of the room, other times executing a scallop-shaped path to try to follow a wall. The overall effect is a random walk. Half an hour later, give or take 10 minutes depending on room size, it declares victory and stops. You can also stop it by picking it up using the built-in handle. A battery charge lasts about an hour and a half.

I tried Roomba on low-pile carpets and hardwood floors in rooms both empty and full. It didn't damage or topple anything, and it did remarkably well at extricating itself from power and phone cords, either by shifting direction or temporarily shutting off the brush. The edge detector—downward-pointing infrared sensors that watch for drop-offs—worked perfectly. Much as I tried, I couldn't entice Roomba to fall down a flight of stairs. I even put it on a table and let it clear off the crumbs.

Roomba slurped up most of the filth, but it didn't replace the need for manual vacuuming or sweeping, and iRobot is wise not to claim that it does. The real Achilles' heel of the robot, though, is the wire that is supposed to keep rug corners from jamming the brush. It got yanked off within a couple runs, and the company had to send me a new one. Even with the wire, the bot didn't like the kilim in our living room one bit. And although it was usually able to free itself from cords, "usually" wasn't good enough: it got hung up at least once per run. You don't have to watch Roomba continuously, but you had better be nearby to help it. I think it's fair to say that Roomba rises above the level of mere gadget—but not by much. What makes it a breakthrough is the price, $200, which approaches the don't-need-spousal-preapproval range.

Roomba closely resembles a vacuum robot, Trilobite, that was introduced by Swedish appliance maker Electrolux in November 2001. Electrolux didn't respond to repeated requests for a demo model and doesn't sell Trilobite outside Sweden, but I tried it out in a shop on a visit there this past fall. Trilobite features a more powerful and rug-friendly vacuum; a sonar to detect obstacles, so it seldom actually makes contact with anything; and a position tracker, so it can return to its home base and plug itself in when it needs a charge. On the minus side, it lacks an edge detector, relying instead on magnetic strips that you lay around danger spots. Worse, its price, 14,000 kroner (about $1,500), is not likely to pass the spouse test.

Watching these robots bumble around gives you a new appreciation for how difficult housework really is. It takes agility, a tolerance for imprecision, and advanced pattern-matching skills—just the abilities with which evolution on the savanna endowed us. Rather than ever making a robot do all that, humans might, I suspect, find the tables turned on them: a future cyborg species could simply hire people to clean their homes for them.

7. "Long-Distance Robots"

by Mark Alpert

The technology of telepresence makes the world even smaller

A week after the World Trade Center disaster, I drove from New York City to Somerville, Mass., to visit the offices of iRobot, one of the country's leading robotics companies. I'd originally planned to fly there, but with the horrific terrorist attacks of September 11 fresh in my mind, I decided it would be prudent to rent a car. As I drove down the Massachusetts Turnpike, gazing at the American flags that hung from nearly every overpass, it seemed quite clear that traveling across the U.S., whether for business or for pleasure, would be more arduous and anxiety-provoking from now on. Coincidentally, this issue was related to the purpose of my trip: I was evaluating a new kind of robot that could allow a travel-weary executive to visit any office in the world without ever leaving his or her own desk.

The technology is called telepresence, and it takes advantage of the vast information-carrying capacity of the Internet. A telepresence robot is typically equipped with a video camera, a microphone, and a wireless transmitter that enables it to send signals to an Internet connection. If a user at a remote location logs on to the right Web page, he or she can see what the robot sees and hear what the robot hears. What's more, the user can move the machine from place to place simply by clicking on the mouse. With the help of artificial-intelligence software and various sensors, telepresence robots can roam down hallways without bumping into walls and even climb flights of stairs.

Until now, businesspeople have relied on techniques such as videoconferencing to participate in meetings that they can't attend. Anyone who's seen a videoconference, though, knows how frustrating the experience can be. Unless the participants are sitting right in front of the camera, it's often difficult to understand what they're saying. Researchers are developing new systems that may make videoconferences more realistic. But there's another problem with videoconferencing: the equipment isn't very mobile. In contrast, a telepresence robot can travel nearly anywhere and train its camera on whatever the user wishes to see. The robot would allow you to observe the activity in a company's warehouse, for example, or to inspect deliveries on the loading dock.

The idea for iRobot's machines originated at the Massachusetts Institute of Technology's Artificial Intelligence Laboratory. Rodney Brooks, the lab's director, co-founded the company in 1990 with M.I.T. graduates Colin Angle and Helen Greiner. iRobot's offices are on the second floor of a nondescript strip mall, just above a store selling children's clothing.

It's the kind of office that an eight-year-old would adore—machines that look like miniature tanks lurk in every corner, as if awaiting orders to attack. The robots are tested in a large, high-ceilinged room called the High Bay, which is where I encountered a telepresence robot named Cobalt 2.

The machine resembles a futuristic wheeled animal with a long neck and a bubblelike head. When the robot raised its head to train its camera on me, it looked kind of cute, like a baby giraffe. Angle, who is iRobot's chief executive, says the company designed the machine to appear friendly and unthreatening. "We wanted to create a device that would be easy for people to interact with," he says. The robot rides on six wheels and has a pair of "flippers" that it can extend forward for climbing stairs. The antenna is fixed to the back of the machine like a short black tail.

After I finished admiring Cobalt 2, I turned to a nearby computer monitor that showed the robot's Web page. In the center of the screen was the video that the robot was transmitting over the Internet. The machine was still staring at me, so I had a nice view of my own backside. The video was grainy and jerky; because the system transmits data at about 300 kilobits per second, the user sees only five or six frames per second (television-quality video shows 30 frames per second). "You're trading off the frame-update rate for the ability to move and control the camera," Angle explains. Transmitting audio over the Internet is more troublesome because of time lags, but users can easily get around this problem by equipping the robot with a cellular phone.

Now I was ready to give Cobalt 2 a road test. Using the mouse, I clicked on the area of the video screen where I wanted the robot to go. The machine's motors whirred loudly as they turned the wheels, first pointing the robot in the right direction and then driving it to the indicated spot. Then I devised a tougher challenge: I directed the machine to smash into the wall on the other side of the room. Fortunately for Cobalt 2, its compact torso is studded with sensors. The machine's acoustic sensor acts like a ship's sonar, detecting obstacles by sending out sound waves and listening to the echoes. Infrared sensors gauge the distance to the obstacles and can also warn the robot if it's heading toward a drop-off. Cobalt 2 stopped just shy of the wall, thwarting my destructive intentions.

The machine that iRobot plans to sell to businesses looks a little different from Cobalt 2. Called the CoWorker, it resembles a small bulldozer—it actually has a shovel for pushing objects out of its path. "It's a robot with a hard hat," Angle says. In addition to a video camera, the machine has a laser pointer and a robotic arm that remote users can manipulate. iRobot has not set a price for the CoWorker yet, but it is already shipping prototype versions to businesses that want to evaluate the technology. The company also plans to introduce a telepresence robot for home use. Such a device could be a lifeline for senior citizens living alone; the robot would allow nurses and relatives to see whether an elderly person is ill or needs immediate help.

Will these mechanical avatars soon be knocking on your door? The fundamental challenge of telepresence is not technological but psychological: I, for one, would have a lot of trouble keeping a straight face if a robot sat next to me at one of our magazine's staff meetings. And can you imagine how most senior citizens would react to the wheeled contraptions? Nevertheless, people may eventually accept the technology if the potential benefits are great enough. For example, an elderly person may decide to tolerate the intrusions of a camera-wielding robot if the only safe alternative is living in a nursing home.

As I wandered through iRobot's offices, I got a glimpse of another telepresence robot called the Packbot. About the size of a small suitcase, this low-slung machine moves on caterpillar treads and, like Cobalt 2, has extendable flippers that allow it to climb over obstacles. The Defense Advanced Research Projects Agency (DARPA)—the U.S. military's research and development arm—is funding the development of the Packbot, which is designed to do reconnaissance and surveillance in environments where it would not be safe for humans to go.

In the aftermath of the September 11 attacks, military officials recognized that telepresence robots could aid the search-and-rescue efforts. So the engineers at iRobot attached video and infrared cameras to the prototype Packbots and rushed them to New York.

At the Somerville office I watched an engineer fasten two flashlights and a camera to a Packbot that would soon be taken to the World Trade Center site.

Although the Packbots were too large to burrow into the wreckage, the iRobot engineers used one machine to search a parking garage. Smaller telepresence robots called the MicroTrac and the MicroVGTV— machines made by Inuktun, a Canadian company that sells robots for inspecting pipes and ducts—were able to crawl through the holes in the rubble. The machines found no survivors but located the bodies of several victims.

This grim task was perhaps the best demonstration of the value of telepresence. As I drove back to New York, I felt a grudging respect for the robots—and for the men and women who'd built them.

8. "Kibbles and Bytes"

by Mark Alpert

How much is that robotic doggy in the window?

A wonderful childlike excitement filled the halls of *Scientific American* on the day that the Aibo ERS-210 arrived in the mail. Clutching the box tightly, I rushed to the office of my colleague George Musser and shouted, "It's here! It's here!" George beamed like a kid on Christmas morning and immediately tore the box open. Inside was a foot-long, three-pound machine that looked like a Jack Russell terrier wearing gray plastic armor. Sony Electronics had bred the robotic dog in its research laboratories in Japan; the name "Aibo" (pronounced EYE-bo) means "pal" or "companion" in Japanese and is also a rough acronym for Artificial Intelligence Robot. For weeks I'd been begging Sony officials to let me evaluate the computerized canine.

In the past few years, toy companies have introduced an entire litter of electronic pets: Poo-Chi the Interactive Puppy (from Tiger Electronics), Tekno the Robotic Puppy (Manley Toy Quest) and Rocket the Wonder Dog (Fisher-Price), to name just a few. But Aibo is the most advanced pooch of the new breed. Sony unveiled the first-generation Aibo ERS-110 in

1999, producing a limited run of 5,000 robotic hounds priced at a howling $2,500 each. They sold out almost instantly, prompting Sony to rush 10,000 similar units to market. The improved second-generation ERS-210, a relative bargain at $1,500, has also won the hearts of well-heeled customers since it went on sale last November.

What can explain such intense devotion? Certainly part of Aibo's appeal is its sophisticated technology. Each mechanical mutt possesses nearly as much computing power as a typical desktop PC. Tucked into the rear of the dog's torso is a 200-megahertz micro-processor with 32 megabytes of main memory. . . . Sensors scattered throughout the dog's anatomy relay signals to the microprocessor, thus mimicking a flesh-and-blood nervous system. To simulate a sense of vision, for example, a transceiver in Aibo's head shines an infrared beam at nearby objects to gauge their distance; this information helps the robot avoid walking into walls. Aibo can perceive colors as well: in its muzzle is a complementary metal oxide semi-conductor (CMOS) imager that gives the dog a 40,000-pixel view of the world.

Aibo's software is equally impressive. Sony designed the robot so that a variety of programs, each encoded on a memory stick, can be inserted in the dog's belly. If you choose the Aibo Life program, for instance, the robot initially acts like a newborn pup and gradually learns how to walk and do tricks. But if you want a fully trained pooch right away, simply pop in the memory stick containing the Hello Aibo program. The catch is that the memory sticks are not included in the $1,500 price; each costs about $90. If you throw in a spare battery charger and assorted extras, the total price can easily run over $2,000.

Perhaps the most intriguing aspect of Aibo's software is that the robot is imbued with canine instincts. We got our first look at Aibo's mercurial character just seconds after George took the dog out of the box and turned it on. (For the purposes of our review, Sony had equipped the machine with a fully charged battery pack and the Hello Aibo memory stick.) In response to George's enthusiastic petting, the mechanized mongrel nipped one of his fingers. The bite didn't hurt—Aibo has no teeth, just a motorized plastic jaw—but just the same, George gave the junkyard robot a firm rap on the top of the head. Aibo has a touch sensor there, and giving it a sharp tap admonishes the creature: the dog is programmed to avoid the behavior that led to the reprimand. Aibo's tail drooped as a sign of contrition, and red LEDs gleamed forlornly behind the visor of the dog's helmetlike head.

By this time several other members of the magazine's staff were peeking into George's office to see what all the fuss was about. Mark Clemens, one of our assistant art directors, cheered up Aibo by gently stroking the touch sensor on its head. Green LEDs behind the visor flashed a happier expression, and a miniature speaker in the dog's mouth warbled a jaunty sequence of high-pitched notes. Then Aibo began walking across the room, stopping every now and then to survey its surroundings.

It was fascinating to watch the robot scramble across the carpet. Each of its legs has three motors, one in the knee and two in the hip socket, allowing the machine to maneuver around obstacles skillfully. As the robot steps forward, it shifts its weight from side to side to keep its balance. Although Aibo's herky-jerky movements have the restless, playful quality of a dogtrot, they also seem vaguely menacing. On seeing Aibo for the first time, many of my colleagues remarked, "It's so cute!" But on reflection several added, "It's also kind of creepy."

Aibo's neatest trick is chasing the pink ball that comes with the dog. Sony has programmed the robot to become terrifically excited when its CMOS imager detects the colors pink or red. As soon as Aibo spots the ball, the LEDs in its tail and visor light up and the miniature speaker trumpets the familiar "Charge!" tune. The robot rushes toward the ball, whirring like mad, until it senses that it's in the right position. Then it lifts one of its front legs and gives the ball a kick. Aibo scans the room to see where the ball went and runs after it again, sometimes butting the thing with its head instead of kicking it.

Some of Aibo's other feats, however, failed to awe me, perhaps because the robot's lifelike behavior had unduly raised my expectations. The machine has two microphones in its head and voice-recognition software that can respond to simple commands. If you tell Aibo to say hello, it will either bow or wave its paw. If you say, "Let's dance," the robot will play a snatch of music and do a four-legged jig. But very often I had to shout the commands a few times before the digital dog would pay attention. Because Aibo is designed to be moody, it won't perform tricks unless it's in the proper frame of mind. Sony says the occasional disobedience makes the machine more lifelike, but I just found it annoying. If you shell out $1,500 for the cur, it should at least show a little respect.

Clearly, my Aibo needed to go to obedience school. I opened the dog's stomach cover and replaced the Hello Aibo memory stick with the Aibo Life program. An old robot can't learn new tricks, I thought, so I needed to work with a puppy. But when I turned on the machine, it just lay on the floor with its legs splayed, making pathetic mewling noises. As it turns out, the newborn Aibo needs at least 40 hours of training to develop into a fully functional adult.

I might have undertaken the task if I didn't have a wife, a kid or a job. But instead I turned back to my computer screen while the baby Aibo sprawled under my desk, crying its little LEDs out. In the end, I had to put the poor creature to sleep. Although the robot is a technological marvel, it didn't hold my attention for very long. Mind you, this is definitely a minority opinion—tens of thousands of customers have each plunked down a small fortune to adopt Aibo. I suspect that it appeals to people who have a lot of time on their hands.

Web Sites

Due to the changing nature of Internet links, Rosen Publishing has developed an online list of Web sites related to the subject of this book. This site is updated regularly. Please use this link to access the list:

http://www.rosenlinks.com/saces/robo

For Further Reading

Arrick, Roger. *Robot Building for Dummies.*
Hoboken, NJ: Wiley Publishing, 2003.

Cook, David. *Robot Building for Beginners.*
Berkeley, CA: Apress, 2002.

Gibilisco, Stan. *Concise Encyclopedia of Robotics.*
New York, NY: McGraw-Hill, 2002.

Levy, David. *Robots Unlimited: Life in a Virtual Age.*
Wellesley, MA: A K Peters, Ltd., 2005.

Lunt, Karl. *Build Your Own Robot!* Wellesley, MA:
A K Peters, Ltd., 2000.

McComb, Gordon. *Robot Builder's Sourcebook: Over
2,500 Sources for Robot Parts.* New York, NY:
McGraw-Hill, 2002.

Predko, Myke. *123 Robotics Experiments for the Evil
Genius.* New York, NY: McGraw-Hill, 2004.

Rosheim, Mark Elling. *Leonardo's Lost Robots.*
New York, NY: Springer, 2006.

Stone, Brad. *Gearheads: The Turbulent Rise of Robotic
Sports.* New York, NY: Simon & Schuster, 2003.

Sutherland, Jon D. *Engineering on the Edge: The
Future of Nanotechnology and Robotics.*
Bloomington, IN: Authorhouse, 2004.

Index

anatomy of, 62–64
collaboration between, 59,
60, 68–70
coupling joint for, 69
designs for, 59–61, 65
limitations of, 58, 65, 66
localization and, 65–68
monkeys, experiments with,
34, 37, 43–45, 47–50,
53, 54
Musser, George, 90, 92

N

National Aeronautics and
Space Administration
(NASA), 23, 25, 27,
28–29
NBLabs, 41
neurons, study of, 37–41,
43–54
neurophysiology, 40, 43
neuroprostheses, 37, 45, 53, 54

O

Observer (Mars), 27, 30
Odyssey (Mars), 30, 32
Ohio State University, 13
Opportunity rover, 31

P

Packbot, 88–89
paralysis, and neuroprostheses,
36–37, 46, 45, 50
PARC (Xerox PARC), 60
Pathfinder (Mars), 27, 28, 31

"PC-Bots," 73–77
Peterson, Kevin, 16, 17
Plexon, 41, 44
Pocket-Bot, 61
Poo-Chi the Interactive Puppy
(robotic dog), 90
Príncipe, José Carlos, 52

R

rats, experiments with,
41–43, 53
Red Team, 5, 9, 11–23
Reid, Ashlan, 51
robots
controlled with the mind,
34–54
for households, 78–83,
87–88, 90–95
miniature, 57–70
for reconnaissance, 57–58, 88
telepresence and, 84–89
Rocket the Wonder Dog, 90
Roomba, 81–83

S

Sandin, Paul, 81
seizures, experiments to stop
with BMIs, 51
Smith, Bryon, 15, 16, 18
Sony Electronics, 79, 90–95
Spirit rover, 24–26, 31, 32–33
Squyres, Steve, 26–30
Srinivasan, Mandayam A.,
35, 36
Stolle, Martin, 17–18